Talking Tidewater

TALKING TIDEWATER

Writers on the Chesapeake

Edited and with a Foreword by
RICHARD HARWOOD

The Literary House Press • Washington College
Chestertown, Maryland

The Literary House Press, Washington College
Chestertown, Maryland 21620-1681

Library of Congress Catalog Card Number 95-082136
ISBN 0-937692-13-1

Cover photo by J. Tyler Campbell.

ACKNOWLEDGMENTS AND PERMISSIONS

The Literary House Press of Washington College is grateful to the authors and their publishers for permission to edit and reprint the works included in this anthology. Some of the original titles (noted in parentheses) have been changed; some of these texts have been edited for this volume.

"A Floating Aria" (excerpted and adapted from John Barth's novel/memoir *Once Upon a Time: A Floating Opera*, Boston: Little, Brown, 1994, copyright 1994 by John Barth) and "Goose Art," (copyright 1992 by John Barth): Both published in *The Washington Post Magazine* are reprinted by permission of Wylie, Aitken & Stone, Inc.

"A Mid-Atlantic Boy" by Jonathan Yardley: First published in *Mid-Atlantic Country Magazine*, 1990, copyright by Jonathan Yardley, reprinted by permission of the author.

"The Colonel" by William Warner: Published in the Nature Conservancy's anthology *Heart of the Land: Essays on the Last Great Places*, Pantheon, 1994, copyright by William Warner, reprinted with permission by the Nature Conservancy.

"The House on the Island" by Anne Hughes Jander: First published in *Crab's Hole: A Family Story of Tangier Island*, The Literary House Press, copyright 1994 by Owen Jander, reprinted by permission.

"Killing Geese," "Water Warriors," ("Saving the Bay") and "Paradise Unreclaimed" ("The Ultimate Edge") by Tom Horton: First published in *Bay Country*, Johns Hopkins University Press. Copyright 1987 by Johns Hopkins University Press. Reprinted by permission of the Johns Hopkins University Press.

"The Last Skipjacks" by Tom Horton: First published in *The New York Times Magazine*. Copyright 1993 by The New York Times Company. Reprinted by permission.

"The Statue Man" ("A Land Unto Itself") and "Pitching" ("Radio Games") by Robert Day: Published in *The Washington Post Magazine*, copyright 1995 by Robert Day, reprinted by permission of the author. "The Linguist" ("Talking Tidewater") by Robert Day: First published in *Mid-Atlantic Country Magazine*, 1990. Copyright 1995 by Robert Day, reprinted by permission of the author.

"A View from the Northern Neck" ("Rappahannock Revisited," "Cemeteries," "Fences," "The Guns of June and July" and "Mollie") by Eugene McCarthy: First published in *The View from Rappahannock County*, EPM Publications, McLean, Virginia. Copyright 1987 by Eugene J. McCarthy, reprinted by permission of the author.

"Bay Blues" ("Chesapkeake Bay Blues") by David Finkel. First published in *The Washington Post Magazine*. Copyright 1992 by *The Washington Post*, reprinted by permission.

"Modern Man" ("Shell Shock") by Bill Gifford: First published in *The Washington Post Magazine*, Copyright 1994 by *The Washington Post*, reprinted by permission of the author.

CONTENTS

FOREWORD

IN THE ESSAY "Goose Art," John Barth ruminates on the "aesthetic ecology" of the Chesapeake Bay and its extensive environs. We are immersed in, and often overwhelmed by, the astonishing output of artists, artisans, novelists, poets, potters, plastic and textile workers, handcrafters, goose and crab memorialists and other aesthetic celebrants of bay life. The quality is not uniform but that is irrelevant to the obvious point that the bay is a great stimulant to artistic and pseudo-artistic endeavor. Whether the supply exceeds, matches or underestimates demand is also beside the point: shelves groan under the weight of the literary output alone; it's all around us.

Our purpose in this anthology is to sort through the abundance of good and bad Chesapeake literature, choose some of the choicest fare and serve it up on a single plate for the pleasure, enlightenment and convenience of readers. It will, we hope, lie well but not languish on your bedside table.

Our contributors are a diverse lot, ranging from John Barth, novelist, critic and distinguished university professor, to Eugene McCarthy, one of the leading public men of mid-twentieth-century America whose essays and poems from Virginia's Northern Neck reveal another dimension of his life and of life in one of the bay's watersheds. Other famous and famously honored authors are represented in this collection, along with young and freshly minted writers on the way to recognition.

Their collective range is considerable. Autobiographical essays in the anthology's first section give us intimations of the influence of oceans, bays, beaches, islands and rivers on the imagination, dreams and self-identity of their authors. The middle section celebrates the human and cultural variety of the region, its customs, traditions and eccentricities. The final essays examine the malign and accidental forces that threaten the health and wealth of the bay and the survival of the distinctive character and lifestyles that have inspired and informed the work of generations of literary men and women.

RICHARD HARWOOD

LITERARY ROOTS

A FLOATING ARIA

On water messages, remembered and imagined

John Barth

MY NATIVE STREET in East Cambridge, Maryland, runs its five small-town blocks from what used to be the East Cambridge Elementary School at its head down to what still very much is the Great Choptank River at its foot. Two miles wide at that point, the river with its brush-grown banks and pebbly beaches called like the Hamelin piper to East Cambridge children as soon as we were old enough to range afield. We played down there in every season, but especially in the endless, subtropical Eastern Shore summers; alone, in pairs, in troops; at games and amusements innumerable, most innocent, some not: Indians and war, tag and Tarzan, desert isle and fright-fraught jungle. We threw oystershells and makeshift spears at neutral targets and at one another; we swam and were stung by sea nettles and rubbed our nettle-stings with sand to make them feel better when we stopped; we fished for perch with bamboo poles, wrestled, sneaked cigarettes and firecrackers, masturbated, killed innocent sparrows and floating booze bottles with Daisy BB-guns and, later, innocent rats and floating booze bottles with single-shot .22-caliber rifles.

Those smashed booze bottles, that weaponry — these were the pre-environmentalist 1930s, the wartime '40s. At the foot of Aurora Street was a fine grassy embankment for rolling down and leaping off and a crumbling concrete seawall for angling and crevasse-jumping. Just downstream was a considerable lumber mill, strictly off-limits but rich in the illicit thrills of trespass, where we climbed the splintery, summer-fragrant stacks of drying pine boards and sprang like superman from stack to stack. Upstream, however, was the heart of mystery, adventure, and treasure: a scruffy, becreepered "jungle" — so we called it — of briers and honey-locusts perched atop an eroding 12-foot bank, cornfield behind and brown sand beach before, crisscrossed with footpaths, embowered with honeysuckle and trumpet vine, and terminating on its upstream end in a spendid unofficial trash dump. Here God had generously provided us with rats and tin cans and bottles and jars for shooting (every male East Cantabrigian was equipped with an air rifle from about age ten till thirteen or fourteen and a .22 bullet rifle after his voice changed) or for floating off and bombarding with rocks and "brickbats," whereof the supply was inexhaustible; it was said that they, like the granite riprap in front of the seawall, were rubble hauled over from the great Baltimore fire of 1904. And in less Western or warlike humors, especially among the more dreamy of us and most especially on my solitary beach prowls, here was the prime place for posting, perhaps even for receipt of *water-messages.*

A note... in a bottle: staple of desert-island cartoons to the present day and motif in fiction back to the eighteenth century at least, from Edgar Rice Burroughs's *Land That Time Forgot* through Edgar Allan Poe's "MS Found in a Bottle" back to Sterne, Defoe, whomever. Before them, Rabelais in the sixteenth century gives us the inverse, a bottle-in-a-message: the flask shaped "Ode to a Bottle" in *Gargantua and Pantagruel*, precursor of the Absolut vodka ad-series in the American 1990s. Earlier yet, in Scheherazades's tales, it is not messages but fearsome *messengers* who pop out of seaborne containers and must be tricked back. In historical fact, pastime of summer-children on tidal shorelines and of shipboard passengers amused to post real greetings, fake urgencies, and hopeful invitations to response from the finder. In historical fact, too, desperate plea and/or last testament of who knows how many hapless sinkers, drifters, strandees — or those in imminent peril of so becoming — for as long as there have been written messages, vessels to sink or strand or shatter, and smaller vessels to float word off in.

Nowadays their high-tech equivalents are the EPIRBs: Emergency Position Indicating Radio Beacons, standard equipment for offshore sailors, which in distress broadcast a locater signal receivable by satellites as well as by passing ships or aircraft; also those transmitters set afloat by oceanographers to drift with the Gulf Stream, say, and mark its chaotic eddies between the Straits of Florida and the British Isles (I do not even mention our Voyager satellite messages to outer space). A dandy find, no doubt, such gadgets, for today's beach-walking counterpart to yours truly in his summer tens and teens, but no more the Real Thing than those toy balloons released by salesfolk, schoolfolk, or celebrators, which — when deflation turns them from aerial to water-messages — become last suppers for pelagic turtles taught by eons of evolution to misread the message. What one yearns for — your solitary preadolescent beachcomber in dreamy search of signs from the world as well as clues to himself — is nothing less or more than a bona fide message in a literal bottle, washed into the Choptank River from Portugal, Chile, China, (although Maine or Florida would suffice), and ostensibly declaring *Here is the key to the treasure* or *Rescue me and I'm yours* but secretly whispering *It is all right. We understand. Things will not always be as they may seem to you now. A quite wonderful life lies ahead for you, comprising not only the best of what you've seen around you thus far but many things of which you can as yet be aware no more than dimly, if at all.* Et cetera.

Heaven knows how many water-messages I myself posted from the rivershore in those summers (always on outgoing tides), most declaring no more than *Set adrift in the Choptank River on May 27, 1941* [say] *by* [myself], *301 Aurora St., Cambridge, Maryland, USA,* but others saying... I don't remember what; all of them, anyhow, announcing *I exist. Here I wait. Give me some sign.* And none — needless to say? — ever replied to. Perhaps they bob about someplace yet in the world's waters, barnacled, beweeded, en leisurely route to wherever, whomever, as their youthful sender floats into his elder decades.

One summer, mirabile dictu, I found one. On the pebbly beach near the jungle dump, in a clear glass gin or vodka bottle not entirely dry inside (I used to cap my own messages tightly for the long haul) and too slimeless outside to have drifted long, it nevertheless bore, by god and in fact, a small sheet of white paper once rolled to fit through the bottle neck and now unrolled to the point of irretrievability except by smashing the container with the usual handy brickbat. Surely my heart beat fast; I can't imagine otherwise, although I half remember an exhilarated calm — *Yes. Of course. At last* — and I was not after all so gone in fantasy as to expect anything more glamorous than *Set adrift off Baltimore*, say, maybe a few days before, maybe from a freighter bound up to the Chesapeake & Delaware Canal or down to the Virginia Capes, but, you know, possibly of Monrovian or Panamanian registry. In fact the message read, in its ink-run, splotched, block-capitaled entirety, IT WAS BILL BELL. Not *If you find this, please reply to*... Not *For a hot time, call*... Not even *I am*... *And you?* Only the cryptic expletive *it* and past-tense copula *was*, quasi-accusatory or confessional, its noun-clause subject unsupplied, and then the ding-dong predicate nominative proper name. *IT WAS BILL BELL.*

Even our thick Cambridge telephone book listed both a *Bell, Wm.* and a *Bell, W.*; I had not nerve enough to call. *What* was Bill Bell? Fifty years later, I still wonder; hence, no doubt, this aria.

The theme of water-messages, I note, itself bobs through my writing, from my first novel (*The Floating Opera*) to my most recent book (*Once Upon a Time: A Floating Opera*). In a 1968 short story explictly titled "Water-Message," the bottled inscription IT WAS BILL BELL becomes the salutation TO WHOM IT MAY CONCERN, followed by the closing YOURS TRULY. "The lines between were blank," reports the narrator, "as was the space beneath the complimentary close" — a blank, it might be said, that my life's labor has aspired to fill. All my books, it goes without singing, are water-messages, posted to whom they may concern, quite as the nameless stranded minstrel in my story "Anonymiad" (also from circa 1968) posts into the Aegean his private versions of the Trojan War, written on goatskin with squid-ink and sealed in emptied amphorae:

"There [he says], my tale's afloat. I like to imagine it drifting age after age, while the generations fight, sing, love, expire. Now, perhaps, it bumps the very wharfpiles of Mycenae, where my fatal voyage began. Now it passes a hairs-breadth from the unknown woman or man to whose heart, of all hearts in the world, it could speak fluentest, most balmly — but they're too preoccupied to reach out to it, and it can't reach out to them. It drifts away, past Heracles' pillars, across Oceanus, nudged by great and little fishes, under strange constellations bobbing, bobbing. Towns and statues fall, gods come and go, new worlds and tongues swim into light, old perish. Then, it too must perish, with all things deciphered and undeciphered: men and women, stars and sky..."

Let's get homely: My wife and I plant messaged bottles on our own Langford Creekshore, to be found serendipitously by young beachcombing grandkids summer-visiting from California (*Help! We love you! G'ma & G'pa*, etc).

Let's get cosmic: What is all literature, if not bottled missives awaiting degustation? Our lives are messages, brethren, by our bodies embottled, afloat in the great sea of the world. We wash up on other folks' shorelines, they on ours. Many go unread, some are unreadable, many are misread, some are read to death, and a lucky few meet their ideal readers. Our Earth is an intricate, lovely message, bottled in its fragile biosphere as in fine crystal and adrift in eddies within eddies of the black universal sea.

Let's get on with it: My Skrip dries word for word as in another tidewater summer I scrawl this latest water-screed, crisp black on clean white, to be bottled between hard covers and posted on the fickle tides of literary fortune. "Borne by currents as yet uncharted," says the "Water-Message" narrator of that story's young hero's find:

"Nosed by fishes as yet unnamed, it had bobbed for ages beneath strange stars. Then out of the oceans it had strayed; past cape and cove, black can, red nun, the word had wandered willy-nilly to his threshold."

Just so, perhaps, figuratively speaking, this aria, to who knows whose threshold; and just so the floating opus that contains it: beach-writing — to be, its author hopes, beach-read.

A MID-ATLANTIC BOY

Jonathan Yardley

WHEN I WAS A BOY of nine my family moved from a suburb of New York City to a very small town in Southside Virginia. This was terra incognita for me, all right, but what it took me a long time to understand was that, to my new neighbors, I was every bit as unknown and mysterious. Every time I opened my mouth I was in trouble: I was a "Yankee," and various characters in various schoolyards took immense pleasure in making me pay for it.

So you would think that I found sweet relief when my family drove north for summer vacations, but a funny thing — I didn't think it funny at all — had happened: Now people in the North thought I sounded like a Southerner, a rebel, a mushmouth. If my tormenters in my new home loved to ride me for the way I pronounced "ball" — "Bwal," they said in mimicry — my friends and kinfolk in my old one tried to tease me into blurting out the "y'all" that somehow had found its way into my vocabulary.

So there I was, betwixt and between. Neither Yankee nor Rebel, but a bit of both. Was I, as in my confused moments I believed myself to be, from nowhere at all? Southerners did nothing to disabuse me of the notion: If you aren't of the South, born and bred, then so far as they're concerned you're from nowhere worth mentioning. Ditto for New Englanders: Good fences make good neighbors is what they say, and their fences are built to keep outsiders out.

So for half a century I wandered back and forth between these polar opposites, coming to terms with both of them yet never managing to develop a strong sense of my own regional roots: a sense that all Americans instinctively long for, born as we are into a vast and heterogeneous nation. Then, quite by accident, an understanding of where I come from — and thus, in no small degree, of who I am — came to me in the summer of 1990, when the telephone rang and an invitation was extended to write the article you are now reading: I am, I soon came to realize, a child of the Mid-Atlantic.

This wasn't exactly an epiphany, but neither was it a phony revelation conjured up for journalistic convenience. Thinking some tentative, exploratory thoughts about this amorphous, ill-defined piece of ground — it certainly isn't a state of mind — called the Mid-Atlantic, I suddenly was struck with the awareness that it is *my* piece of ground. My favorite American writer, the great Mississippian William Faulkner, used to refer to his environs as "my postage stamp of native soil." Well, the Mid-Atlantic is *my* postage stamp.

Consider the evidence. My mother grew up in New Jersey, my father in Maryland. I was born in Pennsylvania, a state settled early in the 17th century by members of my family after whom a town was subsequently named. I grew up in Virginia. I went to college in North Carolina and subsequently lived there for a decade, during which one of my two sons was born. I am now employed by a newspaper in the District of Columbia, and I live in Maryland; one of my sisters lives in West Virginia.

Okay, you say: What about Delaware? Here's about Delaware: Like everyone else who lives in the Mid-Atlantic, I have spent something on the order of half my life on that ghastly fourteen-mile stretch of highway between the Maryland state line and the Delaware Memorial Bridge. Over the years the road has had different names and numbers, not to mention contours and potholes and construction delays, but there has been one constant: It is the bottleneck through which every resident of the Mid-Atlantic must pass en route from one point to another. Delaware is to the Mid-Atlantic as Hartsfield Airport in Atlanta is to the South — as inescapable as death and taxes. To live anywhere in the Mid-Atlantic is to hold honorary citizenship in the First State.

So there you have me: a true person of the Mid-Atlantic. Which makes me — and presumably most of you who read this — a what? A Mid-Atlanticker? A Middleman? A Midler? A Midsectionite? It's a problem, isn't it? Not merely does the resident of this region of ours have trouble defining his region, he has just as much trouble giving himself a name.

Say "Southerner" and you say worlds, conjuring up everything from Faulkner to football, from Memphis to magnolia, from juleps to jazz. Ditto for "New Englander." But say "resident of the Mid-Atlantic," and not merely have you said a messy mouthful, you haven't evoked a single image, except perhaps that of Interstate 95 snaking its noxious course from Rowland in southeastern North Carolina to — yes! — Yardley in northeastern Pennsylvania. Say "Southerner," and in some places you've still said fighting words; say "resident of the Mid-Atlantic," and you've put your audience to sleep.

Maybe it has something to do with being in the middle, a location that rarely arouses much in the way of passion. Good old North Carolina, situated between South Carolina and Virginia, for generations has called itself "a vale of humility between two mountains of conceit," which you could say as well for the Mid-Atlantic, except that it contains the District of Columbia, inside the Beltway of which humility is in precious short supply.

Still, it's true all the same: The Mid-Atlantic is a middlin' sort of place. There's nothing in its history to compare with the legacy of slavery and defeat that still haunts the Deep South, nor is there anything that so vividly reveals a distinctive regional character as did the religious fervors and witch trials that swept through New England during its formative years. "The Land of Pleasant Living" is what the beer commercials used to call the Chesapeake Bay, and the words suit our part of the world just fine: Not "passionate" or "puritanical," but "pleasant."

If you're looking for someone to say that this is bad, look elsewhere. The pleasant atmosphere of the Mid-Atlantic — pleasant climate, pleasant topography, pleasant people — suits me just fine. But it certainly isn't an atmosphere conducive to cultural or artistic upheaval. The great blues singer Big Bill Broonzy once said: "The thing I think about the blues is — it didn't start in the North — in Chicago, New York, Philadelphia, Pennsylvania, wheresoever it is — it didn't start in the East — neither in the North — it started in the South, from what I'm thinkin'." He was thinking right: Can you imagine the blues starting in the Mid-Atlantic?

Of course you can't. "I've got those Wilkes-Barre blues, down to the bottom of my shoes… " Doesn't exactly sing, does it? No, the Mid-Atlantic isn't blues country. It's too diverse, too elusive of pat definition, to have produced the kind of regional sensibility that in turn produces distinctive artistic or cultural movements. Can you imagine a coffee-table book called *Great Country Houses: The Mid-Atlantic Style*? If you can, you've a better imagination — or a better sense of humor — than I.

Yet easy though it may be to laugh at the very idea of "Mid-Atlantic," to make sport of its somewhat artificial arrangement of seven states and one federal district, the truth is that we have a real history and even, perhaps, a real identity.

The first part of it is easy. If you accept the traditional boundaries of the Mid-Atlantic, then the first thing to be said of the Mid-Atlantic is that it is the cradle of American history. Go to the Outer Banks of North Carolina and the Tidewater of Virginia, and you're in the places — Roanoke Island and Jamestown — where the American adventure began. Many of the great battles of the Revolution were fought in the Mid-Atlantic — ditto for those of the Civil War — and it was in Philadelphia that the colonies transformed themselves into a nation.

Having done that, they then chose a capital city, called it Washington, and placed it smack in the middle of the Mid-Atlantic. Two of the new country's first important cities arose in Philadelphia and Baltimore. It was in the latter that, a few decades later, the terrible conflict between North and South boiled down to a painfully divisive and in some respects inconclusive microcosm; torn between the Southern and Northern parts of its identity, Baltimore was racked by divided loyalties just as, in other ways, the entire region was.

Indeed, it's useful to think of the Mid-Atlantic as America in microcosm. In the past the country's conflicts have been fought out here in miniature, just as, today, its prospects and problems are all about us. In the Research Triangle of North Carolina, bursting at the seams with new development — most of it hideous — we have the Sunbelt in miniature. In the steady defoliation of the Maryland and Virginia countryside by suburban developers, we have what seems to be a picture of the American future. In the ruined industrial hulks of Camden and the rotted slums of Philadelphia and Baltimore, we have the costly and explosive legacy of the past.

In these characteristics as in others, the Mid-Atlantic is distinctly and distinctively American; if there's another part of the country in which is contained so much of what defines us as a people, I am unaware of it. It's true that our landscape has none of the West's melodrama and little of the Midwest's monotony, but the land that stretches from our beaches to our mountains is in all other respects paradigmatically American: You couldn't see it in any other country except this one.

It's also, much of it, land of uncommon beauty and character. In the film adaptation of Edna Ferber's novel *Giant*, Rock Hudson travels east from his bleak ranch in Texas to buy a horse. Arriving by train in the Maryland horse country, he's swept away not merely by the horse he will buy or the woman — Elizabeth Taylor — he will marry, but by the countryside itself. The boy from Texas has never seen anything so beautiful — the lush grass, the gentle hills, the rich vegetation, the bright colors — and the memory of it remains with him for the rest of his life.

There's not a place in the Mid-Atlantic that's gone unmarked by beauty. New Jersey, with its hills to the north and its shore to the south. Delaware, with its mighty river. Pennsylvania, with mountains at both ends and incomparable farmland in the middle. Washington, with the great park that cuts through its heart. Maryland and Virginia, with the bay they share and the hills that roll away from it. And North Carolina — if this isn't heaven, why did God paint the sky Tar Heel blue? — with its endless coastline and its magnificent mountains.

We've done a good deal to ruin this landscape, and doubtless our heirs will do more, but so far its beauty and serenity endure, touching our senses and shaping our character. For all the bluster of the region's cities and the pushiness of its suburbs, this is still a quiet and modest place.

You can get a picture of it — a true picture, I think — if you drive down U.S. 29 from Northern Virginia to Piedmont, North Carolina. Yes, this means Charlottesville's gridlock and Lynchburg's dreadful bypass and then the chaos of Greensboro, where the highway suddenly vanishes in an orgy of interstates, but along the way you see the mountains of the Blue Ridge and the comfortable small towns — be sure and take a detour into Lovingston — and the apple orchards and the farms.

It is my favorite drive, one I make several times a year. It takes me through places I know well and love deeply, which is why for me Rt. 29, not I-95, is the main artery of the Mid-Atlantic, the road that takes me where I want to be. Home.

THE COLONEL

William W. Warner

VERY LITTLE in my upbringing seems to have pointed toward a love for our great Atlantic beaches, much less writing about them. I was born and grew up in New York City in a house that was without great books, without a father, and, for some periods of the year, without a mother. In *loco patris* I had only a highly irascible step-grandfather. Colonel George Washington Kavanaugh was his name, and he wanted to be known by all of it. His most frequent utterance to me, apart from constant reminders that I was no blood kin, went something like this: "Your father is a bum, your mother is running around with every gigolo in Europe, so I suppose the spring can rise no higher than its source."

So much for the Colonel, as my brother and I always called him, and the genetic malediction he constantly laid on us. But there was one thing the Colonel did for us for which we are both eternally grateful. Come June every year he took our family, such as it was, to a place called Spring Lake, a summer resort on the New Jersey coast. Not that we especially liked the place. Our schoolmates all went "to the country" on vacations, and Spring Lake with its kiosked boardwalks, well-ordered streets, and great hotels with long porches and double rows of rocking chairs didn't seem very country to us. Reinforcing this impression was an institution known as the Bath and Tennis Club, where our contemporaries spent much of the day playing blackjack and sneaking cigarettes.

But at one end of of the well-ordered streets, beyond the boardwalk and the great hotels, was an immense space. How immense I learned from my older brother, who at age nine or ten gave me my first taste for geography. "Look here," he said, showing me a world map and running his finger along the fortieth parallel, "there is nothing but the Atlantic Ocean between our beach and the coast of Portugal, four thousand miles away."

Suffice it to say that this bit of information, which was quite accurate, overwhelmed me. I soon began taking long walks along the beach, staring out at the ocean and dreaming of the day I might have a boat of my own to venture beyond the breakers and explore it. My brother shared this vision, although more in terms of a quest for better fishing. In due course we therefore built a crude box-shaped scow of heavy pine planking, painted it red, white, and green, and proudly named it the *Rex* after the great Italian ocean liner that was at the time the largest and most luxurious ship in the trans-Atlantic passenger service. With the help of some of our huskier friends we grunted the *Rex* down to the beach. The chosen day was fine, with a sprightly land breeze that did much to calm the breakers. Our plan was alternately to fish and paddle down to an inlet at the south end of Spring Lake that led into a small bay known as Wreck Pond. But after we were successfully launched, our friends all laughing and cheering us on, we found the *Rex* to be something less than seaworthy and quite difficult to paddle. In fact, the sprightly western breeze that had made our passage through the surf so easy was now rapidly carrying us out to sea — straight for Portugal, I could not help thinking — with a strength against which our best efforts were no match. The reader can guess what followed. Alarms were sounded, authorities were summoned, and we were rescued. "One more trick like this and I'm cutting you out of my will," the Colonel said to us when we were brought home, humiliated, by the Coast Guard.

Nevertheless, before the summer was over, my brother and I found we could explore the incongruously named Wreck Pond well enough by foot and bicycle. It was, in fact, what biologists call a complete estuarine system, in miniature. At its mouth was the tide-scoured inlet, constantly shifting its sandy course. Behind the inlet was a shallow bay, a labyrinth of marsh islands, and ultimately, well inland, a freshwater stream fed by a millpond bordered by pin oak and magnolia. Thanks to this complex we could do everything from netting crabs and small fish to stalking the marsh flats looking for shorebirds, muskrat, or an occasional raccoon. We could even catch small trout up by the millpond dam, graciously provided by the New Jersey state fish hatcheries. What a relief these occasions offered from the Bath and Tennis Club, what an escape from the Colonel! Wreck Pond, in short, became our private world.

But there were other worlds to conquer, as the saying goes, in particular a large blank space on maps of the coast which my brother and I had both noticed and wondered about. It appeared as a long finger of land pointing southward, a mere ribbon of land between the Atlantic Ocean and Barnegat Bay. Most remarkably, the southern part of the finger, below a cluster of closely-spaced beach resorts, showed no signs of human settlement nor even a road, so far as we could tell. (The reader will understand how rare this was when I say that even in the 1930s, which is the time I speak of, much of the New Jersey coast was already a solid corridor of resort townships.) The blank space was called Island Beach. It had to be investigated, we agreed.

For this greater enterprise we borrowed a canoe, provisioned it with three days' worth of canned pork and beans, and left an ambiguous note concerning our intentions on the Colonel's pillow. But once again the Aeolian gods did not favor us. This time a wet east wind slammed us against the marshes of Barnegat Bay's western shore, so strongly, in fact, that we found we could only gain ground by wading in the shallows and pushing and pulling the canoe. There was one bright moment in this otherwise dismal effort, however. After rounding a sharp bend in one of the marsh islands we came upon a sheltered and relatively quiet cove. There to our amazement were four or five mink cavorting down a mud slide they had excavated in the marsh bank. Over and over they shot down the slide — head first, tail first, on their stomachs, on their backs — to splash into the water with splendid abandon. Well hidden by the tall cordgrass, we watched transfixed as the mink evidently scrambled up an underwater burrow, reappeared above on the marsh bank, shook their silvery wet coats, and repeated the process. Forever, it seemed, or what must have been at least ten minutes. I have never forgotten the sight, nor seen another mink slide since.

We passed what seemed like a sleepless night huddled under a clump of bushes in the cordgrass that offered little cover from intermittent rains. The next morning we set out again, very tired, under a hazy sun and on glassy calm waters. Island Beach seemed almost in sight on the far horizon to the east, although it was hard to be sure in the haze. Just as we began to ponder the wisdom of continuing our journey, a large and official-looking motorboat with a slanted red stripe on its bow came alongside bearing instructions to take us in tow. "That does it!" the Colonel said to us two hours later when we were brought home again, humiliated but grateful, by the Coast Guard. "I'm cutting you both out of my will."

A few years later, or when I was sixteen and my brother and I had gone our separate ways, I got to Island Beach. I got there in what today is known as an ORV, or off-road vehicle. But mine was quite different from current models. Mine was a splendid little ORV, in fact, for which I make no apologies. Unknown to the Colonel I had acquired a lightweight Ford Model-T beach-buggy prototype with a chopped-down body, painted in salt-resistant aluminum and equipped with four enlarged wheel rims and tires, all for the sum of $50. My buggy was totally incapable of sustained driving in soft sand, having only the standard two-wheel drive and a weak one at that. It therefore could never chug up dunes or otherwise alter the beach topography. To operate it successfully on Island Beach it was necessary to travel at low tide, only, along the wet and more compact swash sand of the forebeach. This meant driving along close to the surf, constantly dodging the biggest waves, in what proved to be a thoroughly exhilarating experience. One could do this, moreover, for ten glorious miles, ten miles of wind-plumed breakers rolling in from the Atlantic, ten miles with seldom another human being in sight. Sometimes there would be schools of marauding bluefish just beyond the surf, marked by sprays of small fish breaking the surface and the screams of wheeling gulls and terns. In such event I would jam on the brakes (stepping on the reverse gear pedal worked even better), grab my cane surf rod, and heave out a heavy lead-squid lure as far as possible. If your cast went far enough, you got your blue. By the time you brought him in and unhooked him, you had to jump back into the buggy and race on to catch up with the fast-moving school. For a boy of sixteen these were moments of pure bliss, of feeling at one with the sea and the sand.

There were other attractions. Often I would leave my fishing companions to their patient pursuits and explore the back beach. The dunes of Island Beach were low, but with steep rampart-like faces on their seaward side. Behind the ramparts were small hollows of smooth sand marked only with the delicate circular tracings made by the tips of swaying dune grass. Then came beach heather and thickets of sea myrtle, stunted cedar, holly, and scrub oak. Gain the highest point of land, perhaps no more than twenty feet above sea level, and the small world of Island Beach lay revealed before you. On the one side were the choppy waves of Barnegat Bay at its broadest, bordered by salt marsh and tidal flats that attracted great numbers of both migrant and resident shorebirds. On the other were the dunes, the white sand, and the Atlantic breakers stretching away to a seeming infinity. It was a small world, easy to comprehend, and I loved it from the beginning.

* * *

New Jersey's Island Beach is what is known to geologists as a barrier island. (The fact that it is not now an island is merely a question of time; it once was and could be again anytime after a hurricane or winter storm washes over its narrow width to create an inlet.) Barrier islands are the dominant feature of our Atlantic and Gulf Coast shorelines and they are found there to an extent not matched elsewhere in the world. They are also the most fragile of our landforms, subject to constant change by wind and water. This is especially true of overwashes, as the storm incursions are properly called, which can both create inlets and move the islands landward. North Carolina's Outer Banks are probably champions in the former regard. The Banks have had at least twenty-five major inlets open and close — six are open today — in their known history.

The formation of barrier islands is complex and still a subject of some discussion among scientists. One of the most common origins, easy to understand, goes by the ungainly name of spit accretion. Picture a relatively straight north-south coastline with a large embayment somewhere along its length. Sand dredged up by wave action from offshore shallows to the north of the embayment will be carried south by a prevailing current. Some of this sand will be deposited when it reaches the slack where the coastline first curves into the bay. The sand so deposited will form a small spit in the same direction. The spit will in turn trap more sand and beach detritus, growing longer and longer in the direction of the current. It may even grow until it completely closes the bay mouth. (This is a common occurrence, incidentally, along the south shore of Massachusetts's Martha's Vineyard island, giving rise to some rather large landlocked bodies of water known locally as "ponds.") Or, what is just as likely, the spit may be intersected by inlets to form one or more barrier islands.

How then can sand dunes build up from what began as low-lying spit accretions? Here wind, not water, is the principal creative agent. Wind blowing sand across the beach will also bring seeds. To begin with, only a few seeds of beach grass need sprout along the beach's driftline. The blades of beach grass will then reduce the speed of the wind passing between them, causing more seeds to drop. More sand will be deposited as well, of course, in progressively greater quantities as the thicker beach grass slows the wind even further. Thus do the dunes grow in nature's form of compound interest. And thus are they rendered more stable, unless man interferes, as the grass roots bind together the sandy subsoil.

Lie down at the crest of a dune in a good thirty-knot offshore wind — enough, that is, to make the sand grains sting against your skin — and you may witness another phenomenon common to barrier beaches. Carefully squinting your eyes, you can see sand flying up from the dune's seaward face and raining down in its lee. What you are literally witnessing is the landward creep of a barrier dune. But here wind is a supporting player. Water — or better, storm-driven water — takes the major role, often generating something more than a creep. The storm overwashes that sweep over barrier islands inevitably add to their landward side by depositing large fans of sand and other sediments which kill the bordering salt marshes and tend to fill up the bays behind them. Some islands have been known to retreat as much as forty meters after a single great storm. Dramatic as such events may be, they do not on the whole contribute as much to landward migration as the ebb and flow, four times a day, 365 days a year, of the tides that race through the islands' inlets. The sand and other sediments carried by these tides are deposited in the form of a fan-shaped delta after passing through the inlets and gaining the quieter waters of the back bays. Thus do the bays fill and thus do islands creep toward the mainland. Some sand, but not as much, will also be taken back out to sea on the ebb tide, in some cases to form dangerous offshore bars. You will notice these dangers on nautical charts, wherever the Coast Guard places the stern warning "CAUTION: Entrance to Inlets: The channels are subject to constant change. Entrance buoys are not charted because they are frequently shifted in position."

Oh, that barrier-island beachfront developers were required to issue a similar warning to prospective clients! It might well read "CAUTION: The properties you are about to purchase are subject to constant attack by the sea. Domiciles built thereon cannot be insured because they are frequently shifted in position." Perhaps this will come in our lifetime, after more and more beach houses wash out to sea.

* * *

Such are some but not all of the ways the barrier beaches of our Atlantic Coast take shape. They are almost as various as the forces that create them. In the north are the wind-driven "walking dunes" of Cape Cod, or the tide-swept and relatively barren Monomoy Island. In the south are the quiet groves of live oak and palmetto of the "sea islands" of South Carolina, rapidly being lost to development, or Georgia's Cumberland Island, mercifully spared by a combination of public and private sources. In between these is the lonely majesty of North Carolina's Hatteras Island, now part of the Cape Hatteras National Seashore. Fifty-five miles long and for the most part pencil-thin, the island lies between the Atlantic Ocean and the broad expanse of Pamlico Sound. Drive down below Hatteras Light to the extreme tip or cusp of the cape (the Cape Point, as it is called, is a highly movable spit) and cast your eyes seaward. For as far as you can see the seas rise up in pyramidal crests and tumble against each other in wild confusion, even in a moderate breeze. But here there are no rocks or underwater reefs. Rather, what you are witnessing is the clash of the Atlantic Coast's two great current systems, or the cold and the southward-trending Labrador Current and the warmer waters of a Gulf Stream gyre. Underneath them, extending twelve miles out to sea, are the shifting sands of the dread Diamond Shoals, known as the "graveyard of the Atlantic." So it was in the age of sail, for some eighty known shipwrecks. Little wonder the sailor's rhyme:

If the Dry Tortugas let you pass,
Beware the Cape of Hatteras.

Little wonder, too, that in this wild setting the Hatteras Lighthouse will soon be moved back from the sea's grasp. Or that the oak frames of old ships, once buried out on the shoals, are periodically exhumed on Hatteras's retreating beach.

Not far to the north of the Outer Banks are the barrier islands of Virginia's Eastern Shore. Starting with the Chincoteague National Wildlife Refuge on Assateague Island, these islands run eighty miles south to Cape Charles at the mouth of the Chesapeake Bay. They are eleven in number counting only the larger islands, and all but two of them are protected by a combination of federal, state, and private sources. At the north is the Wallops Island space-tracking center, whose NASA landlords have at least kept it off-limits to visitors. At the southern extremity is Fisherman's Island, a small national wildlife refuge at the tip of the Cape Charles corridor, where migrating hawks and falcons foregather in the fall before crossing the Chesapeake. In between, or at the heart of this system, are the twelve islands — Smith, Myrtle, Mink, Godwin, Ship Shoal, Cobb, Little Cobb, Hog, Revels, Parramore, Cedar, and Metompkin — that make up The Nature Conservancy's Virginia Coast Reserve. The islands and the adjoining back bay and salt marshes, totaling thirty-five thousand acres, are a meeting ground for northern and southern plant and animal species and thus have a rich biological diversity. For this reason they have been given world-class status, or designation as a United Nations' Biosphere Reserve.

For me the Virginia islands have long held a peculiar fascination. One reason, I am sure, is that getting to them is often an adventure in itself. There are no roads, bridges, or causeways to the Virginia barriers. Rather, you must go by shallow-draft boat and have some knowledge of the labyrinth of marsh creeks, tidal flats, broad bays, and deep-running ancient river courses that lie between the mainland and the outer islands. This area — the back bays, as they are sometimes called — literally pulsates with life. The mud banks of the marsh creeks come alive at low tide with *Uca pugnax,* or the feisty and well-named little fiddler crabs darting in and out of their burrows. Great blue herons or their lesser cousins wait for them at almost every bend in the creeks. Out on the broad marsh you will see marsh hawks circling the hammocks and tumps of firm land. Ospreys dive in the inlets to compete in winter with loons and mergansers. In the fall there will be huge flights of snow geese and brant numbering in the tens of thousands, not to mention the ubiquitous Canada goose and a variety of tipping and diving ducks. Out in the broader bays you will find commercial fishermen dragging for the succulent hard clams and salty oysters these waters offer in profusion. At certain low tides the oystermen will snub their boats to the channel banks, step out onto the bordering tidal flats, and take their pick of the best oysters. These same flats offer prime feeding grounds for oyster catchers and a host of other shorebirds. Willets, yellowlegs, sanderlings, turnstones, glossy ibis, whimbrels, and marbled godwits are always present in season. Other species come in astounding number. Flocks of over a thousand dunlins may be seen in winter, and an estimated six thousand knots have been counted feeding on the larvae of blue mussels on Metompkin Island in the spring.

On isolated sandbars, great egrets and tricolored herons occupy their crowded nests in the shrubs and small trees of the marsh hammocks. Visitors from the south include the brown pelican, white ibis, and Wilson's plover, which nests here at the northern limit of its range. Summertime will also see great silvery tarpon rolling through the inlets, although not in great number, and loggerhead turtles lured from Florida by warming waters. Visitors from the north include the threatened piping plover, which finds the shell fragments of undisturbed beaches much to its liking for nesting materials. Terns — least common, gull-billed, royal, and sandwich — prefer to nest on the berm of the island beaches, not far from the dune line. But the swift-flying Forster, which can hover like a small hawk, will build its nest from the wrack of the marsh islands. Beneath the shallow bay waters are wavy meadows of sea lettuce and other aquatic plants. These underwater meadows are a favored hiding place for the tasty Atlantic blue crab, which searches them out to moult, and a nursery and juvenile growth area for a great many fish, including valuable commercial species that will return to the sea as young adults. The list could go on, the list, that is, of all the living treasures so carefully guarded and nourished in the lee of the barrier islands.

I like best to visit Parramore Island, the largest in the Virginia Coast Reserve, in mid-October. Starting from the reserve headquarters to the south, there is only a suggestion of what is to come. After passing through narrow tidal creeks, a thin dark line begins to appear far out on the horizon. This is Hog Island, seven windswept miles from the mainland across the reserve's broadest bay, now dotted with small flocks of old squaws and buffleheads. But soon there will be the shelter of more tidal creeks and salt marsh as Parramore's mid-island forest comes into view. Overhead are the long V's of Canada geese, flying south. The first snow geese may also have arrived, and ducks are everywhere, wheeling and turning in the clear autumn sky, or dropping down swiftly to marsh potholes. After landing on Parramore's bay side, one traverses a pond-studded salt marsh and enters a forest of loblolly pine, surprisingly tall for being so close to the sea. The air is cool and quiet, and the carpet of pine needles makes walking easy. An inquisitive deer may approach you, completely unafraid, as if wondering where you fit in the island's scheme of things. Migrating warblers flit overhead. But soon, very suddenly, you break out of the forest near the ruins of a Coast Guard lifesaving station. There is the ocean. And there is the beach, the broad and gently sloping beach, and the long rows of breakers rolling in from the Atlantic.

At this time of year you may want to look for the long wavy lines of scoters beating their way south just beyond the breakers. Or be on watch for the rare peregrine falcon rocketing down to Cape Charles. Or you may simply want to train your binoculars in either direction, as far as vision will carry, until there are only mirages where sand, sea, and sky come together in a common haze. To pause, that is to say, and gaze at Parramore's endless beach. There are not many like it. Pray God it may remain so.

* * *

Thinking back, I sometimes wonder where or to whom one should express gratitude for the rich experience our national seashores and other coastal reserves so generously provide. In my case thanks would have to begin with New Jersey's Island Beach, scene of my boyhood awakening and still preserved, wonder to say, by the state's Department of Environmental Protection. Or perhaps even further back to Wreck Pond, Spring Lake, and, yes, even the Colonel. So I will say a word to him now, in a form of address I never used in his lifetime. Namely, thank you, Grandpa, for getting me into all this. And thank you, too, Grandpa, for getting me out, in another sense, at a very critical moment. On that day long ago when my brother and I were drifting rapidly toward Portugal in the *Rex,* it was you, after all, who called the Coast Guard.

A HOUSE ON THE ISLAND

Anne Hughes Jander

Fifty years ago, the Jander family abandoned its harried suburban existence in Connecticut and moved to tiny isolated Tangier Island in the Chesapeake Bay. Their friends thought they were trying to "escape." In fact, they were rediscovering a life distilled to the basics: work, responsibility, friendship and love. This excerpt from the memoir Anne Hughes Jander wrote a few years later brings a unique culture back to life.

BECAUSE OF AN ICE STORM we found Crab's Hole. In February of 1943, a sleety rain turned to ice and clung heavily on the branches of trees throughout central Virginia, at the same time spreading its shimmery danger along all the roads leading out of Fredricksburg, where Henry and I were on an early lap of a winter's holiday. We were traveling without a car because of the gas restrictions of those wartime days and had planned to venture by bus to Charlottesville and thence back to Williamsburg. Since the ice storm forced us to abandon our goal of visiting Jefferson's Monticello and the University of Virginia, we made our way by delayed trains to Williamsburg, which we discovered had changed from the peaceful town we had once known to a horribly busy military camp center, in and out of which swarmed the wives of hundreds and hundreds of Seabees and Navy officers. Optimistic as usual, we had made no reservations and so were compelled to sit up all night in the lounge of the Williamsburg Lodge, grateful as puppies to be let in from the cold.

We were certain that somewhere in this area there must be a quiet spot the Army and Navy hadn't taken over, a place where we could vacation for a few days. So we got out a map and studied it closely. What we eventually found was a small island, shaped like a fishhook, almost in the middle of Chesapeake Bay: "Tangier Island."

"Let's find out what that island is like," proposed Henry — and I quickly seconded the idea. It was only with considerable determination that we were able to discover the complicated itinerary involving reaching the place. By ferry, by bus and by taxi we arrived at Crisfield, Maryland, from which small port, we had been told, one could take a small mail boat out to Tangier Island. We reached Crisfield in the late afternoon, only to discover the mail boat had already departed. By this time, our spirit of adventure had been aroused; and so we spent the night in a tourist home, and the next morning exploring the oyster-shucking and crab-picking houses down by the wharves.

Eulice Thomas, the genial captain of the Tangier mail boat, not only agreed to our request to sit out on the deck for the two-hour ride across the bay, but even joined us for much of the way, leaving his wheel to one of the passengers who were enjoying a much warmer crossing in the small cabin.

"Quite a lot of folks come over here to see our island in the summertime," he said. "Not many in the winter, though, once the ducking season's over."

We had been watching what was first just a speck on the horizon grow and grow until we could distinguish a tall church steeple and finally many white houses set close together along what appeared to be one long street. Cap'n Eulice corrected us, however, and said that there were two long streets running parallel, the farther one hidden from the sight of boats entering the small harbor. Following a series of channel markers, we neared the island. As the boat drew close to the wharf and we alighted, we were subjected to stares from a dozen or more youngsters of various ages who were there to meet the mail. Several men were on the dock with large two-wheeled pushcarts, and we loitered long enough to see the carts loaded with boxes of groceries for the village stores, bags of feed and coal and the bags of U.S. mail and parcel post.

Cap'n Eulice, in response to our queries about lodging for the night, directed us to the home of Cap'n Josh and Miss Amanda Pruitt. "They're a nice couple, and they take in roomers. Anybody will show you where they live."

He was correct. As we walked down the very narrow street, lined on both sides with white houses, each one proudly displaying its small lawn neatly outlined with a whitewashed picket fence, we were ushered along by kindly villagers who finally pointed out a somewhat larger house to be that of Cap'n Josh. I think we should have known without their help, however, for seated in a chair on the lawn, behind the fence, was an old gentleman whose face we couldn't have forgotten had we never glimpsed it again. Enjoying the warm Virginia sunshine on a pleasant, late February day, he sat surrounded by billows of filmy white fishing net. In his hands was a hook that he used to attach the net to a stout rope. He was in his late seventies, we judged, with snow-white hair and a strong, firm face on which the years had left only a gentleness that was evident also in his voice.

"Excuse my sitting down," he asked, "but it is hard for me to get up nowadays. If you'll just go right in, my wife will take care of you."

At our knock came Miss Amanda, somewhat bent in figure but with a youthful face and smile. The warm sun of outdoors wasn't present in the hall, but we followed our hostess to a cheerful upstairs room where she lighted a small portable oil stove and invited us to be comfortable. We paid her in advance for the room — the amazing price of 50 cents apiece per night.

In the afternoon we walked the length of the main street, past the four principal stores, the post office and the small moving picture theater. Folk whom we stopped to question were willing to vouchsafe information, and we learned that the electricity on the island was produced by a small plant that couldn't give twenty-four-hour service but provided current only from 5:00 in the afternoon until 10:30 at night. As we reached the end of the street — which, by this time we had been told, was called a "ridge" — we crossed over a long strip of marshland, broken by canals, one or two running longitudinally and the other extending from these to the ridge we had just left and to the one we were approaching. The other ridge was less closely built up, with houses on just one side of the path. On this ridge, the "West Ridge," the path was of clay, rather than the strip of asphalt surface on the "Main Ridge." As we finally meandered again over the arched bridges that crossed the canals at the opposite end of the island and came once more to the white fences of the Main Ridge, we were in time to see the lights suddenly twinkle forth up and down the island's length.

We went to bed between soft flannel blankets instead of sheets. Warm and cozy though we were, it was a long time before I fell off to sleep. I kept thinking of John Crockett and his wife, who had come here back in 1686 with their family of eight sons and daughters, whose descendants now numbered almost a third of Tangier's inhabitants. And my mind pictured the figure of Parson Thomas, the distant ancestor of Cap'n Eulice, whose thunderous sermon of warning to the British encamped on Tangier in 1812 had, according to Cap'n Josh, proved a true prophecy of their failure to take the city of Baltimore.

The big event of the day on the island, we discovered, was the arrival of the mail boat. Next afternoon we joined the group of eager children on the wharf to greet the returning people who had been over to Crisfield to do special shopping. As we walked back toward the village, we chanced to enter into conversation with a pleasant, open-faced woman of perhaps forty-five years.

"Do you mind if we walk along the road with you?" we asked.

"Indeed I don't," said the woman, who introduced herself as Lenore Crockett. "I like to talk to strangers who come on here. Have you been to the beach yet?"

"No, we've wondered about that... whether you could get to it without a boat."

"If you'll walk as far as my house, it's just a little farther on to the bayside; and I'll take you over there if you'd like."

We assented eagerly. Again crossing the marsh on the path we had followed the previous day, this time we continued down a side lane past half a dozen houses or more, and then along diking built, our new friend told us, by the British many years ago over a strip of rather muddy marshland. Suddenly the beach was before us. In both directions it stretched as far as could be seen. Accustomed as Henry and I were to the rocky shores of Connecticut's beaches on Long Island Sound, we were delighted by all that sand; and we walked some distance along the shore. Looking back toward the island's houses, we noticed a rather dilapidated house at the southern end of West Ridge, separated from the rest of the ridge by a stretch of vacant land.

When we drew attention to the charming location of this house, Mrs. Crockett remarked, "That's a place you could buy if you wanted to."

Henry and I exchanged a somewhat meaningful glance.

Cap'n Josh had invited us to attend a prayer meeting that night. Instead of being held in the big white church, it was conducted — in an effort to conserve fuel — in the small hall belonging to the lodge of the Daughters of America. Perhaps 75 people were there to hear their minister explain passages of scripture and to spend a few moments in prayer. The hymns were sung with great gusto, somewhat slowly and with considerable freedom of style, but with much joy and fervor. The meeting was about to be disbanded when Cap'n Josh stood up to speak. "Friends," he said quietly, "we have with us tonight a couple from off the island who seem to like our town very much, and I would like you all to meet them. Before you go, will you all stop to shake hands with Mr. Jander and Mrs. Jander?"

As they left the hall, one and all came to us and shook our hands so earnestly that again our hearts were touched. I didn't dare look toward Henry lest he notice the shine of tears in my eyes.

* * *

The little house on the southwest end of the island proved to be difficult to obtain — a sore trial to my impatient nature. Having fallen in love with Tangier, I was in a constant dither lest someone else get the house before we did. Four years later, such fears might have been well founded, for even isolated Tangier Island was to feel the postwar housing shortage. At that time, however, there were no returning veterans and their brides to consider. The little house we wanted was separated from the other houses on the ridge by a good 500 yards; and Tangier women prefer to be close to their neighbors. Furthermore, the house was located about a mile from the main docks. Tangier watermen, we learned, understandably like to be near their boats. They arrived early in the morning, sometimes in the blackness of night if the tides demand it, to go to their crabbing fields and oyster grounds. A long walk to the dock is nothing they relish. To make our chosen house still more unpopular, it had been owned previously, we found, by a very energetic man who, in addition to tilling the few acres that surrounded the house, had made and sold coffins. The little building in which the coffins had been stored was still there — and was supposed to be haunted.

We had visited the island first in the month of February, but it wasn't until the following October that we discovered definitely who owned that house. In the meantime we had brought our youngest son, Mark, then 9, to spend a few weeks in the home of Eulice and Hattie Thomas and their young son, Rudy. Hattie and Rudy then came up with Mark to visit us in Connecticut that summer. Finally, a letter came from Hattie informing us that some people from Baltimore had expressed interest in the property. The next afternoon found me on Tangier Island, having dropped everything to save "my house" — as I now thought of it — from the grasp of the Baltimoreans.

The owner of the house, it had been determined, was Captain Peter Williams, an active businessman of the village; and so, accompanied by Hattie, I paid a call on Cap'n Pete that very evening. He was a small, energetic and pleasant old man, with a most kindly wife, whom Hattie called Miss Rose.

"Sit down, sit down," said Cap'n Pete, as he drew chairs up for us. "What do you want of a house way down there at the end of the West Ridge? Wouldn't you prefer one up this way farther?"

"No, Cap'n Pete," I said, forgetting all the rules of bargaining. "I've fallen in love with that particular spot, and I've persuaded my husband to buy it, if you'll sell, and if the price is reasonable." I was breathless in my eagerness.

"Well," said the old gentleman. "I wouldn't be able to say right now whether or not I would sell it, but I tell you what I'll do. I'll think it over."

Next evening found Hattie and me again at Cap'n Pete's home. After preliminary small talk, he said, "I've decided that if you really want that house you can have it. It's not much use to me; and my foster daughter who's been living there wants to move somewhere closer to the dock." Whereupon he quoted a price that was well above what Henry had given as the limit we should pay.

My spirits dropped and my eyes filled with tears. Feeling about as silly as I could, I rushed Hattie out with me to the cover of darkness, where I could cry in comfort.

The following morning I said a discouraged farewell to Hattie, and walked with Eulice to the mail boat. There we were met by Cap'n Pete, who drew me aside.

"My wife says I should let you have that house for what you feel it's worth. I didn't have any idea you wanted it so badly; but Rose thinks maybe you and your husband will be a help to the island if you come down here to live. So when you come with your husband next time, tell him to come to see me. I'll not sell the house till he comes." I could have hugged the old gentleman — and very nearly did.

All the way back to Connecticut on the train Cap'n Pete's words echoed in my mind: "... if you come down here to live." We had pictured ourselves going occasionally to the island for a rest from the everlasting race of life that is the commuter's lot. But "to live" had never entered our minds.

Within me I knew that, in Westport, we were not truly living. The telephone began ringing in our house often at 6 in the morning — and continued till late at night, interrupting practically every meal. Henry's occupation as a builder had made him the property of architects and clients. Even his Sundays were no longer his. We had both become involved in clubs, church work and choirs. Our four children at one point attended four different schools, which necessitated membership in four separate Parent Teacher Associations. I made sandwiches for teas, sold tickets for benefits and served on hordes of committees. Our evenings, if there weren't some community or church meeting to attend, were consumed in a constant round of parties and obligatory entertaining. We had many and good friends, but rarely had time to have any but the most hurried chats with them. The children went to music lessons, to dancing school, to Girl Scouts and to Boy Scouts. And because we lived a mile from the center of town, I had become a taxi driver for a large part of every day.

Live? This was not what I believed life should be at its best; yet here was time fast slipping away — the years with our children growing fewer, and middle age creeping up on us.

By the time the train had pulled into Pennsylvania Station all was settled: We were going to pull up roots and move to Tangier. At that moment there remained but the necessity of persuading Henry — which, from experience, I sensed might be easily accomplished.

* * *

Our oldest son, Kent, chanced to be home on furlough from the Army when the actual date of departure arrived, so he and Henry went on ahead with the jalopy to arrange for the transport of the furniture from Crisfield to Tangier. It was left to me to supervise the emptying of the house and to follow the moving van with the remaining three children, Owen, Mark and Sylvia, the dog, the cats and our old Buick.

It would be an understatement to say that I was grateful to arrive at Crisfield. There were Henry and Kent, who had managed to hire a boat for the furniture. It really wasn't hired, however. Young Charlie Pruitt, a friendly and handsome Tangierman who had married a school teacher from off the island, needed a new roof for his house and had made a deal to provide his boat in return for the assistance of Henry and Owen in the work on his roof, which turned out to be a satisfactory arrangement all around. Fortunately, the day was calm and nothing was even dampened on the ride across Tangier Sound to our new home.

For the last hundred yards of the voyage everything was transferred to the small skiff belonging to Parker Thomas, whose services we had previously engaged for clearing the water bushes from our land. There was no lack of help. Every small boy and girl on the island, it seemed, was present; and no sooner did a new load arrive at Crab's Hole landing — we had, by this time, named our house in honor of the countless fiddler crabs who made their homes on Tangier — than dozens of small but willing hands were there to carry things on the last lap to the house.

Our small grand piano caused a sensation — it was the first of its kind ever to appear on the island. The fact that its legs could be removed was astounding to the onlooking children. When the men had finally reassembled the instrument there was immediate demand for music. There in our small living room, strewn now with boxes and barrels, we held the strangest concert in which we had ever participated. Owen at the violin; Henry, Sylvia and Mark singing; with me accompanying them with hands still black with the grit of moving tasks. We could have had no more appreciative audience than the kindly watermen who were to be our neighbors and the curious children who crowded about us.

Having deposited his family and furniture at Crab's Hole, Henry left for New York the next day. There were innumerable odds and ends to be finished up in the dissolving of a business partnership of more than 20 years' standing; and with four children to assist me, it was assumed that the task of settling shouldn't be too difficult. We had blithely entered on a life of relative pioneering, and now the test was upon me. For water there was only a small rain-water cistern, the contents of which would soon be exhausted. An empty cistern meant carrying all our water from the pump at Miss Sadie's, about 200 yards up the West Ridge. Though there was a sink installed in its proper place in the kitchen, it as yet had no running water. We had managed to find some kerosene lamps and already owned several candlesticks, but quickly discovered that there was no use in lighting them to enable us to work at night since there were as yet no screens on our windows and doors. Even the tiny glow of a candle brought a zestful swarm of mosquitoes to feed upon our foreign flesh. This same lack of screens had already invited millions of flies into our house. The neighbors assured me that the mosquitoes were quite bad because of a recent rainy period; but since no special mention was made of the flies, I assumed that they were just the regular occurrence. To help things along, real summer weather came early that year. We had no icebox, and milk that was carried the long mile from Homer Williams's store had to be drunk almost instantly to keep it from going sour. Butter swam in the butter dish. We were hot and thirsty by the afternoon of our first day's attempt to bring order into our new home, and we were without ice even to cool the lukewarm water.

All day long children came to watch the progress we were making with the house. They came not individually, nor yet in groups of two or three, but in gangs of 15 or 20. We were all so anxious to be welcome in the community and to be found friendly that we went out of our way to be entertaining to our ever-increasing guests. We played the piano and violin, exhibited the various rooms of the house and explained who would sleep where, and chatted as pleasantly as our tired backs, mosquito-chewed arms and legs and thirsty tongues would allow. Sometimes there would come a lull. As the children sat with me in the bay window of the dining alcove, we could glance back through the kitchen window at the winding path crossing our land from our neighbor's property.

"Another contingent is approaching," Owen would announce — and groans would go forth from us all.

At dusk on the second night I practically crawled upstairs to bed. For the first time I allowed myself to wonder, "Has this just been one horrible mistake?" A strong southwest wind was blowing, and the surf on the bay was so noisy that it seemed to be beating against the very windows of my bedroom. The sound of the wind and water merely lulls me happily to sleep nowadays, but that night it added only dreariness to my heart as I stifled my sobs from the ears of my children, whose unhappiness I feared might be as great as my own.

Next day I awoke with the old Welsh stubbornness again to the fore. Leaving Sylvia to manage the last ends of unpacking with the aid of her brothers, I caught the mail boat for Crisfield. There I made a purchase that was destined to bring us more comfort than anything I had ever bought in my entire life: an ancient, green enameled icebox that I straightaway arranged to have delivered at the wharf. Next I invested in a big hand sprayer and a gallon of insect killer (the days of DDT, beloved DDT, had not yet come).

Miracles were beginning to happen.

Next afternoon there arrived on the boat the window screens that Henry had obtained for the house. Kent and Owen, having been provided with careful instructions from their father, managed by nightfall to install at least one screen per room. With the new sprayer, every inch and corner of Crab's Hole had been cleared, temporarily at least, of mosquitoes, and all the flies had been swatted. That evening we were able to light our kerosene lamps, and all of us gathered around the dining room table to read by that soft light in peace.

* * *

The house at Crab's Hole originally resembled nothing more than two big boxes attached to each other, the one slightly taller than the other. No shutters adorned the naked windows; there were no ells or porches to soften the severity of its high lines. It had been built by Severn Crockett, son of Noah and grandson of Risley, more than forty years previously, from materials salvaged from the ancient house of his grandfather, which had been located some hundred yards to the south. The beams and framework were very old, as were some of the floors. Henry, with his experienced eye, had said at once that the body of the house was sound and free from rot. By the time our family moved in, its lines had been changed significantly by the addition of bay windows on the south end of the living and dining rooms. These two bay windows were one long extension and between them there was room for a tiny entrance hall and a small coat closet. The dining room-kitchen had been glorified by the addition of a built-in sink, counters and cupboards along the entire northern wall, and the living room boasted a fireplace, which was the only functioning fireplace on the island. (We have since learned that a number of the older houses of Tangier do indeed have very old fireplaces that have been plastered over as the more modern coal and oil-burning stoves came into popularity.)

The old floor in the living room we painted black; and contrary to the advice of our neighbors, we didn't cover it with either a hardwood floor or the customary linoleum rug used on the island. As a result, we have suffered with cold feet in the wintertime; but we are able to point with pride in the summer to our original floorboards and to delight in the beauty of their uneven surfaces, ridged from years of wear and sanding. Tangier houses cannot have cellars due to the costliness of making them waterproof, and so they are built on low piers of brick with an airspace beneath to prevent the rotting of the timbers. When a fierce no'wester is blowing across the bay the wind sweeps through the cracks in the floor, lifting the small scatter rugs by a half-inch above the old boards. By February of each winter we are almost persuaded that we should swallow our pride and succumb to the modernity of a hardwood floor.

Soon after moving in we built a two-story addition on the north of Crab's Hole, which gave us a large room upstairs. Ultimately, when

Tangier gets its envisioned town water system, this will become a bathroom and storeroom; for the duration, however, it now houses a 900-gallon tank for the collection of rainwater from the gutters installed around the roof. The first floor of the addition is a summer kitchen, milk pantry and general junk room. By gravity flow we are able to run water from the upstairs tank into the sink in our kitchen below, and into the little bathroom into which we converted the small closet under the stairs. In this tiny bathroom, along with a toilet and sink, we even have a shower, bought from "The Book" (as the islanders call the Sears Roebuck or Montgomery Ward mail-order catalogues). The toilet we use only rarely, since we discovered that it put too great a drain on our limited water supply. We continue to take the journey to the little privy that stands in a lonely spot on the dike that encircles the Crab's Hole property.

Since the outdoor privy is inevitable, we determined that ours at Crab's Hole should at least have individuality and a degree of respectability. Hence it was painted red with white trimmings to match the house, and, within, Henry built a neat little magazine rack to satisfy the peculiar habits of certain members of the family. On the south side is a big window offering an expansive view across the marsh to the distant shore of Chesapeake Bay; and opposite that an equally large mirror. The little red outhouse we felt must have a name; and so we called it "Bermuda." ("I'm off to Bermuda!" is the family way of putting it.) Our privy is indeed an altogether private place; and since one of its finest views is toward the east — especially lovely in the early morning, at sunrise — we are all of us in the habit of enjoying our stays in Bermuda with the front door wide open.

To make the northern extension look right architecturally, its roof was extended to include a small kitchen porch, but the construction of the brick floor for it was postponed. A year or two ago, all of the family being at home for six weeks or so, it was decided that the time had come not only to finish that brick floor but to build the long-desired screened porch on the west end of the house, looking out toward the bay. The porch construction went along fairly rapidly, but the work on the floors of the two porches was a tedious task. First of all, the boys ferried sand in the skiff from the beach, making fully three dozen trips. While Owen and Mark took over the sand job, Kent did the excavating and the transferring of the topsoil gained thereby to the low areas of the lawn. Next he built a sustaining wall along the other outer edge of the excavated area from concrete blocks surmounted by bricks. It seemed that the sand never would fill up the space, but at last it was time to lay the bricks. None of the boys had ever tackled such a job before, but under Henry's expert guidance they managed fairly well. Owen mixed the cement, stopping frequently to repair to the living room to listen to his beloved phonograph records, to Kent's utter disgust.

"Will you please make that brother of mine attend to business, Mother?" was a common request that summer.

When the screened porch was finished, its handsome brick floor had the proper slope toward the sides to carry away the rains that might beat in from the sky. The result was just beautiful! We could scarcely wait for the cement to dry between the bricks before moving in the porch chairs and the old homemade table and benches that had been patiently waiting in the coffin-house to be put back into use.

Over the bay window in the kitchen there was a place that looked rather bare after we had completed the painting of the walls. It begged for something to perk it up, but pictures didn't seem quite right for the spot. "It needs a motto or a rhyme," Henry and I agreed; but it was several days before we hit on anything to suit us. Finally I found a couplet by William Henry Davies; and Henry, with a narrow brush, lettered in blue the words that sum up appropriately our feelings as we sit together in the bay window lingering over our meals:

What is this life if, full of care,
We have no time to sit and stare?

One of the reasons why it is fun to be poor is that one never can get all the work that an old house needs done at once. If it were possible to hire plenty of labor, and haul in materials without thought of cost, of course the rapidly attained results would be quite thrilling — but not nearly so much fun as when they are achieved in gradual steps. Each little closet that Henry builds for us, each coat of paint that goes on the walls, brings with it a special sense of achievement and joy. How much more pleasurable when things are not finished in one fell swoop — and there's always something new to look forward to.

Already I am planning for an attic floor with a disappearing stairway, so that the parade of friends whom our children are always inviting can be more comfortably bedded down. I'd like a new fence for my rambling roses to grow upon, and a brick walk to the house with tulips bordering it.

* * *

Now that Tangier streets are aglow with electric lights, and now that we have but to push a button again to bring the wonders of electricity into our home, it is fun already to reminisce about the three-and-a-half years when we lived in comparative darkness. Those years were an experience that I would not have lifted from my life. When I open the kitchen cupboard and glance at the row of kerosene lamps on the top shelf, filled in readiness for the day when a storm may temporarily put the electric plant out of commission, I am conscious of a feeling of tenderness for them as for old-and-true companions.

At any rate, I am willing to forget the tedious daily task that was mine to fill the lamps and trim the wicks and polish the chimneys. When we first came to Tangier I could never seem to remember this job until it was time to light the lamps. Filled they could be at the last minute, but I discovered early that glass chimneys could not be tardily washed since they would crack if used before completely dry. Day after day I would do a makeshift job with a piece of tissue paper, feeling guiltily envious of the shining lamps of my neighbors. At last I hit upon a solution for my forgetfulness. Efficiently, I had arranged a place for my lamps on a shelf inside the big kitchen closet, where they were hidden from my sight. Then the remembrance came to me of the mantel in my grandmother's home, where in view of all she kept her row of pink, blue, green and white glass lamps. Ours were not pretty, or made of lovely hobnail glass as were hers, but nevertheless, I decided that they should be placed daily on a little table beneath the kitchen clock, in full view. Thereafter I needed but one morning caller to catch me with my lamp chimneys blackened, and the oil in the lamps unreplenished, for me to reform my ways.

The task of caring for the lamps eventually became a matter of pride too. The morning dishes were washed and dried as quickly as possible; and then, with plenty of piping hot water and soap, the chimneys were sozzled and resozzled in the suds, rinsed quickly and polished with cloths made from old feed bags — which left the least amount of lint and made the glass sparkle.

When I first began to trim the wicks of the lamps, I was reminded of the woman who, in an effort to straighten the line of her lawn hedge, trimmed and trimmed until the hedge disappeared. The art of making a slick, clean slash at the carbon came after much trial and error.

The reward of all this came at twilight, when I could smirk with pride as Henry lit the evening lamps, which now sent out their straight, steady flame within their shining chimneys, giving to our supper table a soft and happy glow. I recall with special affection our first winter on Tangier, when Sylvia, Owen and Mark were all attending school on the island (Kent was off in the Army), when I was doing substitute teaching, and Henry was already exploring the possibilities of a project to create a new power plant. On the cold, dark, windy evenings of January and February, the only room we could properly heat in our house was its large dining room-kitchen. With all the lamps in the house collected in the middle of the dining table, the children gathered around and did their homework, I did my class preparations and Henry worked on his extensive correspondence. The cats would curl up on the sofa, and the dog slept under the table. For a couple of hours the family rule was, minimum conversation. All this togetherness in the magical embrace of the light and the warmth from our assembled kerosene lamps! Indeed, those were moments that none of us in our family would ever lift from our lives.

When we first came to Tangier the town did have an antiquated electric plant that produced direct current. Tottering with age, it was unable to work full time; so, as we discovered that first day on the island, the electricity was turned on about five o'clock in the afternoon, then switched off again rather promptly at 10:30. Because of the low voltage and the direct current, which necessitated special equipment, only a small percentage of the islanders had their homes linked to these power lines. Electricity not being available during the morning and afternoon, electric refrigeration was of course out of the question. The wires were strung on low poles, and in many stretches the insulation hung loose from the wires in strips that dangled in the breeze. The poles had not been set very deep, and during every storm several of them would predictably fall across the narrow streets. When the old engine gasped its last, about a year after our arrival, there were few tears shed. Missed most of all were the street lights, which though few in number and very dim, did help a bit to make walking safer at night.

Henry was aware of the important work that had been accomplished by the Rural Electrification Administration. The REA had been founded back in 1935, its specific mission being to bring electricity to communities so remote that they could not be serviced profitably by private companies. Realizing that Tangier Island was precisely the sort of community that this agency had been created to benefit, Henry early had the dream of bringing Tangier to the attention of the REA. Having been elected a member of the town council, he found the other members equally anxious to see Tangier equipped with a modern plant, and so an appeal was made to Washington. Representatives of the REA made an initial survey; but to our chagrin, they reported that Tangier's population was not sufficiently large to warrant the construction of an electric plant here. And, they further reported, it would be entirely too expensive to connect the island with mainland plants by means of a cable. Hence, there seemed but one solution: to construct a town-owned plant, and either to supplement its cost of maintenance by money-raising schemes, or to charge a very high rate for electricity consumption. The town was too poor to take on the burden of borrowing the amount needed, and so the council asked for contributions to a newly created "Electric Fund" in the form of shares, to be paid back with interest later on.

The watermen of the island at this time were more prosperous than they had been in many years, due to wartime prices for seafood; but they remembered all too well the hard days of the Depression, and so were reluctant to part with their money for what seemed to many a reckless and crazy plan. Some argued that their money would be lost, as it had been in several unfortunate business ventures attempted on the island in earlier years. Others voiced the opinion that they had done without electricity all their lives, and could continue to do so. There were, as always, some few with vision and with faith — and the contributions of these people were sufficient to enable the council to proceed with the installation of poles and lines, and with the construction of a small building to be used as an office and to house two electric generators, obtained from government war surplus stock. Then in December 1946, the council came up against a stone wall. Transformers, ordered several months before, were still unavailable. We ourselves sent pleading letters to everyone we could learn about who was in any way connected with the manufacture of transformers — but to no avail.

Henry and I spent a couple of months that winter in Williamsburg. While we were there the REA held its annual convention in Richmond, and Henry decided to attend it, entertaining the faint hope that some of the REA cooperatives might just have some extra transformers that they could lend us until our order came through from the manufacturer. This hope was quickly eliminated. Still, as a result of that trip, undertaken on the spur of the moment, came electricity for Tangier Island.

Early in the spring came a blessed letter from the REA, saying that Henry's earnest plea for transformers and his picture of the seriousness of our situation had, in fact, spurred several of the engineers to make a further study of our island's need. By chance they had discovered that Smith Island, our neighbor to the north, had made a similar request for REA assistance some years before — and had likewise been turned down. Now it seemed to the engineers that a combination of the two islands — thus doubling the number of potential consumers — might be feasible.

To shorten a long tale, the town sold its plant and equipment to the REA, and there was created "The Chesapeake Islands Electric Co-operative." From this new enterprise, just before Christmas of 1947, electricity was generated for Tangier Island.

As it began to look more and more certain that power would actually be sent through those wires that had been strung (but remained so long unused), and after the shareholders in the original venture had received checks for their shares — plus interest — one by one the objectors became silent. When finally the power switch was turned on, all were loud in their requests to have their homes wired for electricity.

Oh yes, there were still criticisms — new criticisms. Some said the streets were now too brightly lit. One woman complained that her electric iron was much too hot. I myself had become so unaccustomed to electric appliances that I likewise burned my fingers on the toaster and the waffle iron and so added my own complaints to the others, facetiously. Luckily the arrival of electricity on the island coincided with the appearance on the market of more and more appliances — after long years of wartime shortages. Nowadays, when the mail boat arrives each afternoon it has become a common sight to see washing machines, refrigerators and electric stoves being lifted to the dock. Two of the town's stores have become agents for well-known appliance manufacturers. And now, we note, a common pest on the mainland has appeared on Tangier, in the form of the vacuum cleaner salesman, who has found our island to be fertile soil for his sales talk.

We in our family, in all our years before we came to Tangier, had been so accustomed to the modern conveniences that go along with electricity that we never imagined the possibility of being thrilled by such things. Now, however, again and again as we touch a switch we are indeed thrilled — and take joy in our appreciation of how our lives have been changed. It is such fun to watch the vacuum cleaner sucking up all that sand that is forever being tracked into our house. We have revived one of our favorite family rituals from Connecticut days: the Sunday night supper of waffles. We understand the amusing "complaint" of one neighbor, that since the coming of electricity her bread bill has soared, because her family wants toast at every meal, just for the fun of watching the bread pop up out of the toaster.

* * *

Tangier Island has long been a target for newspaper reporters. An unsolved murder, the mischievous and disorderly pranks of restless youth — such things are common enough happenings all over the country but take on an added interest when reported from an island. Journalists have reported tales of the clannishness of the Tangier people and have shown pictures of their homes and of their narrow streets, with certainly no intention of being unkind. Occasionally, however, items have been included that have seemed to the island folk to imply ridicule. The result has been a strong antagonism for all publicity, which is unfortunate, since the people have in their customs and manners here, and in the strange beauty of their town, a unique way of life of which they can be rightly proud.

First of all, we residents of the island should proclaim afar our freedom from the noise of the automobile. The only encroachments of modern transportation on Tangier's streets are the town tractor and a few motor driven scooters. An automobile can pass with difficulty along the main street, can turn only at the very end of the mile-long road, but, of course, cannot possibly pass another car. Hence, its usefulness here is minimal. The town tractor has already been put to good use in the transportation of coal and other heavy loads, and may eventually be the means of a program of garbage collection — at present an acute problem on the island both from the standpoint of the town's beauty and of its sanitation. But the whir of automobile motors, the screeching of brakes and the accompanying danger that automobiles produce for pedestrians are lacking on Tangier, and this very lack is one of our greatest blessings. True, there are disadvantages in having to attend a meeting on foot on a very rainy night, but we Tangiermen solve that problem simply enough by remaining at home. After all, there is always another night for the meeting.

Much has been made in published articles of the remnants of old Elizabethan speech in the language of the Tangier community. Not having any knowledge of early language, I am unable to judge to what extent this is true, but even to the unpracticed ear there are certain words and phrases that appear in the speech of the older people (though these are gradually disappearing) and certain vowel pronunciations that are certainly of early English origin. Our old friend Parker Thomas's speech was packed with unusual words, and I wished after his death that I had written them down more faithfully. He spoke often of being "sob wet" — an expression that mystified me, until I found it listed in our Merriam-Webster Unabridged Dictionary among English expressions now obsolete. Parker frequently used the word "we're" for "our" as in, "We were getting we're boats tied up." He would go to the dentist to have a tooth pulled, he assured me, after the swelling had "suaged" — which I found to be the obsolete dialectic English form of "assuaged." He called the small seat in a rowboat a "thaught," which likewise I found to be the old form of "thwart," the nautical term for such a seat. For a long time I thought that the common pronunciation "drudge," for the harrowing of the ocean beds for crabs and oysters, was merely a mispronunciation, and that the Tangiermen had used it to indicate the labor involved. This I also found to be an obsolete and dialectic form of "dredge." I once heard a Tangier woman say that her father was a "great hand to prog." "Prog" is a very old word indeed, and orginally meant "to pick up a living by begging or thieving." As used on Tangier the word came to mean "picking up clams or oysters, or catching some fish when food supplies were low."

Parker always spoke of "neighbors" as though the word were spelled "nibors" — with a long "i"— and of the "niles" he was hammering, and of the "siles" of a boat. Then at times he would say, "What iles (ails) that?" meaning, we came to learn, "Isn't that strange, though?" This pronunciation of the long "a" vowel sound is standard on Tangier Island, for old and young — just as to this day it remains standard on the British Isles among people of the working classes.

The short sound of the vowel "a" is likewise somewhat changed by the Tangier tongue. To the little children who shout their greetings as we go along the path to Crab's Hole we are not Mr. and Mrs. "Jander," but Mr. and Mrs. "Jiander." When they have a scrap with one another they are "miad"; and when they do something wrong they are "biad" boys.

One of the most interesting customs of speech is what the islanders themselves call "talking over the left." This consists of saying, in even the simplest remarks, the exact opposite of the meaning intended. Just as it is not unusual for people elsewhere to say, "Well, this is a nice day!" — on a very rainy morning — Tangier folk will employ this speech mannerism at all times. If I wear a pretty dress for the first time, a child will say to me, "That's a poor dress," or should it be raining pitchforks, he will comment, "It ain't rainin' none." Only by the subtle tone of voice can one ascertain the true meaning, and after almost five years of residence on Tangier I still occasionally confuse the message.

Substituting in the high school the first winter after we moved here, I had numerous embarrassing experiences, until I learned to recognize whether the pupils were answering normally or speaking "over the left." "That's an easy lesson" meant it was an extremely difficult one. "Yes" often meant "no."

Older people on the island, when they play this trick of language, will often say something like this: "I had a poor visit — over the left." The younger people, however, are so familiar with this habit that they find no need for the old signal. Inquiring among the Tangier folk for the origin of this custom, I failed completely to trace it. People of the age of sixty or younger claim that they cannot remember when the custom didn't exist. Folks of seventy-five or so insist that they did not use it as small children.

I think that perhaps I have found, by accident, the mystery of the "over the left" twist in Tangier English. One day I was visiting a historic home in Richmond and fell into conversation with the curator of the place, a woman of some 60-odd years. Telling her about the island and some of its delightful customs, I chanced to mention "over the left" speech, and stated that I had been unable to find out how it began. She recalled that when she was a child living near the James River, this usage was common among young people. A form of slang, she considered it. Like other slang expressions, it had its day, as she recollected, and then passed from the speech of the people in that region. We both decided that perhaps Tangier watermen, fishing or oystering in the James River, had acquired this usage and brought it home to the island. For some unknown reason — perhaps a desire to conceal their true thoughts from prying strangers — the people of Tangier cherished the custom, and made it a part of their everyday language.

* * *

A recent issue of *Life* magazine contained brief resumes of the experience of some eight couples who had "escaped" from city life to the country. In a later issue, one of the letters to the editor, written by a Mr. Baird Hall of Waitsfield, Vermont, pointed out that these people had made a decision that was almost the reverse of escape. They felt, he said, "the urge to come to grips with responsibilities — economic, social, political and philosophical." At the time of our move to Tangier there were those who hinted that perhaps our venture was simply an escape from responsibility. This now seems very funny to us, for had there been even the slightest thought of "escape" in our plans — and we don't like to admit that there was — the responsibilities that we left behind now seem so materialistic, and so commonplace, compared with those we have taken on since coming to Tangier. Though at that time we would have been somewhat embarrassed to have confessed that we hoped to lead a more useful life on Tangier than we had been living in Connecticut — and though we would have been the last to proclaim that we were driven by any such mighty urge as Mr. Hall suggests — it is in fact true that the words of Cap'n Pete's wife, Miss Rose, had a considerable influence on our decision:

"Maybe you and your husband will be a help to the island if you come down here to live."

Now that sufficient time has elapsed for any evidence of our influence to have become manifest, a completely honest facing of the facts would probably reveal that most of our hopes in that direction have been in vain. Henry can undoubtedly be safe in assuming a certain credit for the electrification project. He could not have accomplished it single-handed, to be sure, and the assistance of his fellow council members was indispensable; but his ability to organize and his perseverance were at least helpful. I think too Henry would like to pat himself on the back for having brought the tax lists of the town into something approaching order. Because of the similarity of names on the island, and because of the failure of past generations to record their property deeds at the county courthouse, a tremendous mix-up had developed over the years; and only weeks of tireless work on his part, involving much questioning of the older inhabitants of the town and the postmaster, whose work makes him familiar with names of the people, plus much checking of old records and innumerable visits to Accomac, the county seat, brought any kind of order to this chaos. As a builder, too, Henry has had opportunity to be of assistance to the islanders at times. Certainly, the appearance of built-in kitchen cupboards in the houses of some of the people can be traced to the interest provoked by those that were installed in the kitchen of Crab's Hole. As for my own influence, except for the fact that a few children can now play the piano a little, and several groups of high school youngsters have seen New York on pilgrimages I've conducted to the Big

City, the horrible truth is that I've had none — unless the fact that a number of women who formerly never drank hot tea, but have acquired the habit through association with me, can be considered an accomplishment.

However, if our life here among out Tangier friends hasn't resulted in the "good" that Miss Rose so optimistically imagined it would, it certainly has been worthwhile for us. This statement is made in spite of the facts that when I substituted in the high school here for a year I lost 17 pounds that I couldn't well spare, and that recently a physical checkup showed that Henry, now in the years of middle age, will do well to rest more than we have in the past. True, we have both worked harder physically on the island than we ever did in our New England home. But the missing 17 pounds were regained in short order at Crab's Hole, where the daily rest I needed was interrupted by no phone calls nor salesmen ringing the doorbell.

All that, however, is but the physical side. What really matters is not whether we are a little thinner or a little weary at times but that we have learned so much here. We know that big things don't happen overnight. We came here with enthusiasm and optimism to spare, certain that the school on Tangier could be brought to the standard of the best rural schools of the nation within a few months at the most. We saw the need for electricity and for running water, for a library, for better recreational facilities for the youth of the island, for a medical and dental clinic, and for better adult education.

To date there is electricity on the island and now there is talk of running water in the not-too-distant future; and a library, after four years of persistent effort, is in the final throes of birth. A parents' organization is working on the creation of a new playground for the children. These few improvements have taken the combined efforts of the council, the church and the school for several years. The other hopes we nurtured so happily are a long way yet from accomplishment, but we ourselves have learned to be patient.

Along the way, too, we have lost all the false pride we have had.

Had the disappointments we encountered through the months been insufficient to erase it, the numerous strange tales about us — mostly critical — that reached our ears would have completed the job. These tales, many of them false, most of them unkind, but a few of them well- founded, not only destroyed our foolish pride but also much of the sensitiveness from which both of us had been previously unaware that we suffered. Dick Elliott, onetime pastor of the church we attended in Connecticut, and a person we were blessed to count among our friends, used to say that sensitiveness was truly but selfishness. Here on Tangier, where every word we have spoken and every move we have made has been well hashed over, we have come to know the truth of Dick Elliott's words.

Indeed, there have been rough spots in the past years. They are at once forgotten, however, and sink into oblivion every time that Henry and I return to Tangier after an absence of even just a few days. The 20 minute walk from the dock to Crab's Hole extends into an hour or more. First, we must stop at the electric plant to see if Junior Moore, the efficient young manager of the cooperative, has been getting along all right. All down the ridge we are met by those who we know by now are our true friends, who inquire about the children if we have been off visiting our youngsters, or who simply say, "I've missed you both going by!" We know they are sincere, for they say the same to those who were born on the island. We know that they miss us as they would an old shoe, for they have now accepted us as part of the everyday life of Tangier. Sometimes we must stop on the way home to deliver articles we have bought in the city for various housewives. If our return has been anticipated, we are often met with a plate of fried oysters or crabs, just to help out with our supper, and sometimes we are invited to Elizabeth Pruitt's for one of her good meals. Miss Nora or Miss Sadie will perhaps be standing by their fences to greet us, and Doris will run out to assure me as I pass that our pets, whom she's been feeding during our absence, are all right. As we cross the bridge over our deep canal, the red siding and the white shutters of Crab's Hole come into view, while dog and cats run madly toward us, beside themselves with joy that we are back again. And together we philosophize as we drink the necessary cup of tea and look out over the marsh, peaceful in its late afternoon solitude. Always we conclude again and again that the people who have known us at our weakest as well as at our best are, in the long run, the closest of our friends.

CULTURE

GOOSE ART

John Barth

DURING MY LIFETIME, and particularly in the decades since World War II, the tide of interest in the Chesapeake Bay region — popular interest, "media" interest, literary and general artistic interest — has risen very considerably, for better and for worse. My wife and I lately saw, but did not eat at, a place called something like the Baltimore Oyster House in San Francisco, where Chesapeake Old Bay Seasoning was also available in area markets. On the menu in Tokyo's Imperial Hotel we saw, but did not order, Chesapeake soft-shell crabs (we had not gone to Japan for crabs). There have been Chesapeake Bay National Geographic photo essays and PBS television documentaries; there are innumerable Chesapeake Bay gift-and-souvenir shops around the watershed purveying Chesapeake Bay calendars and cookbooks and sweat shirts and seasonings and every other merchandisable gizmo that can be caused to bear some item from the now-standard iconographic repertoire: wild ducks and geese, blue crabs, oysters, cattails, oyster-dredging skipjacks, screwpile lighthouses, et cetera ad infinitum, perhaps ad nauseam. Over in Cambridge, Maryland, my native town, a young microbrewery brews both a Wild Goose Amber beer, not bad, which I have seen for sale in Seattle, and a Thomas Point Light lager complete with screwpile lighthouse and red steamed crab on its label (the old Thomas Point Light is just below Annapolis). There are professional Chesapeake folk singers and folk talers and wildfowl decoy carvers and other tidewater arts-and-craftsers.

And there is, if not a flood, at least a vigorous stream of Chesapeake writing, ranging in kind from the texts of Chesapeake Bay coloring books and cruising guides and videocassettes and coffee-table photo albums, through feisty ecological polemics (Tom Horton's *Bay Country),* Pulitzer Prize-winning natural-historical/sociological ruminations (William Warner's *Beautiful Swimmers),* and blockbuster commercial novels (James Michener's *Chesapeake),* to capital-L Literary fiction — enough to justify, in May of 1992, the first-ever Chesapeake Bay Writers Conference. Sponsored by the Chesapeake Research Consortium, the Solomons Environmental and Archaeological Research Consortium, and other estuarine interests, it convened for three lively days on Solomons Island, where the Patuxent River meets the bay, and comprised historians, folklorists, environmentalists, and photographers, as well as writers of fiction and verse.

What is one to make of this abundance, this rendition of "Chesapeakery" into various artistic media — besides a few bucks, if that's one's game? The two simplest-minded reactions, I suppose, are these: On the one hand, a kind of blanket anathema, such as some of us feel toward waterfront real-estate developers. When the skipjack and the blue crab and the screwpile lighthouse attain the status of commercial logos, that circumstance may be taken as a fairly reliable sign that the way of life they vaguely symbolize (in some cases, even the boat or beast or building directly represented) is passing from vigorous, unself-conscious existence into merchandisable nostalgia, or has already so passed. Contrariwise, one might simply welcome and be proud of this "development" of our regional "image," which has put our home waters — native home to some of us, adopted home to ever more millions of others — increasingly on the map of national and even extra-national awareness. I had the interesting experience in Stuttgart recently of presiding over a two-week seminar of young literature professors from such former communist-bloc countries as Romania, Bulgaria, Hungary, Czechoslovakia, even Albania, as well as a few from what at the time was still the Soviet Union; our seminar topic was fairly high-tech and had nothing whatever to do with tidewater Maryland, but out of curiosity I asked how many of those bright young men and women had some sense of what and where Chesapeake Bay might be, and Maryland's Eastern Shore. Remarkably, more of them than not had at least an approximate idea of the place (how many of us can say the same of the Strait of Otranto or even the Sea of Marmara?). Even more remarkably, considering the scarcity of Western-bloc literature in the regimes that these young scholars had grown up under, a fair fraction of them knew of the place not only from their general geographical sophistication but also from having heard of (in a few instances from having actually read) either Michener's *Chesapeake* or — excuse me, but I was surprised and delighted — some novel or other of mine. No doubt they had been politely prepping for their Stuttgart seminar.

I have said that these two contrary radical attitudes are the simple-minded ones: "Get that schlock out of here!" on the one hand; "Look, Ma, we're an industry!" on the other hand. In fact, I have a sneaking sympathy for both hands, especially for the former. Every cruising sailor knows the sinking feeling, so to speak, of having a favorite little-known secluded anchorage "discovered," whether by a developer or by the cruising guides and sailing magazines. There are certain prize spots that some of us won't even tell our fellow sailors about lest word get around. My wife and I are delighted that handsome Langford Creek (off the Chester River, across the bay from Baltimore), where we live, is described in one of the standard Chesapeake guidebooks as "unimpressive." We wish they had added *Submerged piles; sharks and shoaling reported; beware of the dog.* Yet, like many another, I have been bonded since childhood to the tidewater scene, and I've spent much of my literary working life trying to wrestle what I feel about the place into prose sentences for other people to read. When, therefore, as sometimes happens, some Japanese or Brazilian or Romanian writes to tell me that she or he hopes to visit one day the scene of my fiction, I am duly gratified — while at the same time recognizing that in my small way I have become part of the problem.

With that recognition comes a loss of innocence that is the end of easy, simple-minded attitudes toward various exploitations of the bay, including its aesthetic exploitation; and in that loss of innocence is the beginning of real-world complexity, if not inevitably of wisdom. If it were in my power, I would no doubt prohibit all further "development" of tidewatershed real estate for the next generation or two, and take action against lots of other contributors to the ecological and scenic despoliation of the bay and its surroundings. But I cannot make that high-minded pronouncement from any comparably high moral ground, for not only do the Barths already safely *have* their bit of creekside real estate, but it happens to sit in a more or less failed subdevelopment — thank heaven for such failure! — a former cornfield (former woods and wetlands, if you go back a couple of centuries) latterly called "Langford Bay Estates." We wince at the pretentious name, for there is not much of a bay there, just dear, "unimpressive" Langford Creek — beware of the dog. The modest houses thereabouts, our own included, are so far from being "estates" that the first time my wife and I sailed up that way, twenty years ago, we noted in the ship's log that the creek was "quite impressive ... except for a clutch of tacky little houses at its fork." For the past dozen-plus years, one of those ... unassuming little houses has been us.

The analogy holds, I believe, with the Chesapeake artsy-litsy scene, which is also a growing number of us: I mean the moral complexity, the *complicity* even, involved in our more or less artistic *use* of the bay — one more strain on the cultural ecosystem. In a general way, I am turned off by the overload of commercialized, touristical Chesapeake nostalgia; by the ubiquitously merchandised images of what I'm lucky enough to be able to see, live and for real, by looking out of my windows, and have so seen — except for a 20-year expatriate interval "up north," during which I began to write novels set in tidewater Maryland — literally since the day I was born, in what is now called Dorchester General Hospital, on the south bank of the great Choptank River. For some while after we moved back to the Old State Line, the Barths had a rule prohibiting any Chesapeake motifs in our house or aboard our boat (where we don't allow any nautical motifs either): no Chesapeake serving trays, cocktail napkins, place mats, pottery, parquetry, et cetera — on the grounds of image-overkill. It had been another matter up in Pennsylvania, up in New York, up in Massachusetts, where I treasured my Aubrey Bodine Chesapeake photo albums, my first editions of Gilbert Klingel and Hulbert Footner and Paul Wilstach, my tidewater maps and charts. But to surround oneself with images of one's beloved when one is in her embrace — that's a touch redundant, no? Not to say kinky.

Well, that admirable house rule of ours lasted for a while, but it was eventually undone by two exemplary subversive factors, which I shall call the Pedagogical and the Aesthetic. Out-of-state houseguests and grandchildren and others sometimes need it explained to them just where they are when they're sitting on our porch or perching on our bowsprit; nothing like a cartographical cocktail table or serving tray or a handsomely framed hydrographical chart to facilitate that bit of instruction, or indoctrination. We have even, on occasion, identified certain ducks out on our unimpressive creek by consulting the hand-painted wildfowl tiles around our fireplace; those somewhat corny but ornithologically correct tiles came with the house, and are a handier reference than Roger Tory Peterson if we happen to be duckwatching from that particular room. And when cruising the bay, we often plan our day's run over breakfast with the aid of certain cartographic place mats under our bagels and coffee — more convenient for that purpose (despite their clearly posted warning against using them for navigation) than the large-scale nautical charts on which we'll do our actual course-plotting as we go along.

That's the Pedagogical Factor — more of an excuse than a justification for our having the stuff around. The truly operative factor is the

Aesthetic one. To the question that I posed a while ago — the question "Why should anybody, other than a tourist or an expatriate, clutter up the house with more or less expensive *renditions* of Tidewaterland (graphic and plastic renditions, literary and musical renditions, whatever), when the real article is all around us?" — the answers are (1) that even junk renditions have more than mere souvenir value: They are affirmations, however crude, of esteem for the things depicted or symbolized, like Baltimore Oriole and Washington Redskin emblems; and (2) that a truly artful rendition has a value, even a reality, transcending the value and reality of the thing rendered. A living, breathing, honking Canada goose in flight over the Eastern Shore marshes is one thing; we may value it as a handsome wildfowl, as an element of the ecosystem, as meat on the table, even as a symbol of Chesapeake Bay country from September through March. A junk rendition of a Canada goose may still serve that symbolic function, rather like a bumper sticker exhorting one to HONK IF YOU LOVE THE CHESAPEAKE. But a *splendid, marvelous* rendition of that goose-in-flight into photography or paint or poetry or perfect prose is more than just a reminder of the real thing or a secondary symbol of what the real thing may symbolize for us: It is a real thing in itself, a noteworthy addition to the stock of apprehensible reality, and it may be prized as such even by people who know and care little about our particular piece of geography; by people who may never have heard of the place.

I have written about this factor elsewhere and won't dwell on it here. Gift shops in Holland, for example, are as full of souvenir wooden shoes and images of tulips and windmills and canal boats as our tidewater shops are full of all the stuff I've been speaking of, at every level of taste — and the second largest pool of customers for that merchandise, after the tourists, is the Dutch themselves, who as a people are evidently quite fond of their windmills and canal boats and tulips and *klompen;* they enjoy affirming that fondness in replicated images even while surrounded by what those representations represent. Their countryman Rembrandt was fond of those things too, and he rendered them so well (along with other subjects) that people go all the way to the Amsterdam Rijksmuseum to see the Rembrandts without necessarily even bothering to check out the local countryside that inspired him.

That's what I mean by the Aesthetic Factor. Together with the Pedagogical Factor and the Bumper-Sticker-Affirmation Factor, it accounts for our house's being just about as full of Chesapeake Bay stuff as any of our neighbors' houses. Indeed, one room of our place we have come to call, with some embarrassment, the Goose Room, by reason of the high wildfowl-image count therein — more accurately, the high wildfowl-and-other-tidewater-image count. With the same mild embarrassment, but without embellishment, I offer now a far from complete inventory of those images, in order to get to the argument of this sermon:

The fireplace duck-and-goose tiles I've mentioned already; they came with the house, and were painted by a woman down the road who exhibits her work in Chesapeake arts-and-crafts shows. Not bad, not great; we ourselves would never have bought and installed them, but there they were. It would have been too aggressive, too unneighborly (and too expensive) to tear them out and replace them with something more to our taste, something iconographically neutral: and so we pretend that they're sort of useful for duck identification — and there's the entering wedge. The light-switch plates in that room have duck and goose decals on them — really kitschy. Those too came with the house; in this case, however, we could easily and inexpensively have replaced them. So why didn't we? Well, they happen to resonate in a campy way with those fireplace tiles, so what the heck: We name it the Goose Room, and in it we hang a series of marine-architectural drawings that my brother gave us one Christmas, years ago — structural drawings of Chesapeake bugeyes and skipjacks and log canoes by Howard Chapelle and R. Hammond Gibson. That same brother then picks up on the idea and gives us the following Christmas a stylized, varnished-wood half-model of a goose in flight that looks like a streamlined hybrid of the Lufthansa and the old Ozark Airlines logos; we mount that over the doorway and balance it on the opposite wall with a nifty black-and-white photograph of a stalking heron by Skip Willets, playing off the abstraction of the one against the finegrained realism of the other. Next thing we know, there's a 2-by-5-foot heron parquetry in the next room, and a foot-high heron or crane sculpted out of Hindu sacred-cowhorn on the windowsill, and a two-goose Japanese brush-drawing yonder, and a giant full-color photographic blowup of a she-crab over the mantelpiece of the goose-tile fireplace, and on and on and on — including several shelves of literary Chesapeakia ranging from the 1930s WPA Writers Project guide to the Old Line State (re-edited in 1976 by Edward Papenfuse and republished by the Johns Hopkins Press) to Warner's *Beautiful Swimmers* and Klingel's *The Bay* and Horton's *Bay Country* — all the usual suspects. Meanwhile, out on the unimpressive creek itself, so many live specimens are rafted up that we suspect we've decoyed them in with all that goose art, and we fantasize some Alfred Hitchcock culmination wherein feathered Reality swarms into the Goose Room from off the flyway and overwhelms Art, leaving our house in the condition of our waterfront lawn in winter, all goose down and goose dung. The real thing.

Let me see now whether I can salvage some relevance from the litter of this (partial) inventory; maybe even mold from these goose droppings my cultural-ecological argument. To begin with, I do not propose, at least not on this occasion, any hierarchy of categories. I do not assert that a work of "Chesapeake" literature by Christopher Tilghman, say (of whom more presently), or for that matter by Ebenezer Cooke (colonial author of the original "Sot-Weed Factor" satire) or Capt. John Smith or Daniel Defoe (I'm thinking of the passage in Defoe's *Moll Flanders* in which Moll crosses the bay from the Potomac to the Nanticoke in rougher weather than any she ran into in her transatlantic voyages) — I do not say, just here, that any of these is inherently "better" than a Chesapeake Bay coloring book or cruising guide or souvenir videocassette. They're in different categories, not to be ranked against one another. Likewise the mallard-and-cattail mailbox in front of our property (it came with the house, I swear) versus the big Audubon blue heron reproduction in the entry hall, for which we're responsible (it echoes the trim paint — Williamsburg blue). There is no *versus* involved, for the reason that John Audubon and the anonymous mailbox artist were up to different things: ethological accuracy combined with compositional beauty in the Audubon, crude recognizability combined with merchandisability in the mailbox. "Let a hundred flowers blossom," said Chairman Mao Zedong once upon a time; let a hundred and one cattails grow, and ospreys wheel, and herons stalk, and wild geese honk along the mainstream and tributaries of our estuarine art.

This sweet nonjudgmentality is Proposition One of my ecological argument. It need not apply, however, *within* the several categories. Indeed, it *ought not* to apply (this is Proposition Two), for that way lies the anarchy of indiscrimination. It is one thing — a quite okay thing — to enjoy almost equally a terrific American cheeseburger and a terrific item of French *haute cuisine*, depending on the occasion. It is quite another thing, and not okay at all for our cultural health, not to recognize the difference between a terrific cheeseburger and a mediocre or abominable cheeseburger; between a terrific and tasteless *suprême de volaille*; or between those goose-art light-switch plates, which are accurate but tacky; those goose-art fireplace tiles, which are also pretty accurate and maybe just a touch tacky but not uninteresting in their overall composition and in the artist's carrying of the figures across the separate tile-lines in a number of places — and that black on white *sumi* brush-drawing of a brace of honkers crossing a full moon, which is arguably the least "accurate" in ornithological detail but of immensely more artistic interest precisely because so much Gooseness and Full-Moonhood are suggested there with such a radical economy of means and virtuosity of touch.

The *sumi*, in short, is not mere goose art; it is art that in this instance happens to involve geese as its subject matter. It is "about" geese, for sure, but it is by no means *simply* about geese, in the way that those decal'd light-switch plates may be said to be. It is also about the medium of ink and paper, the craft of brush drawing, and the *sumi-e* tradition of rich suggestiveness in a few masterful strokes. In a word, it is capital-A Art, and although my interest in it is not altogether pure (the drawing hangs where it hangs because its subject happens to be geese), I could just as readily admire it if I didn't give a honk about geese. Indeed, in another room on the premises is a *sumi* rendition of crab apple blossoms, even more artful than the geese but relatively unconnected with matters Chesapeake. It's there just because it's terrific.

That's enough about the subject of aboutness, which indeed I've written about before, using crab art instead of goose art to make the point. My argument here is that while we need not and ought not to make comparative judgments about crab apples and oranges, let's say, we owe it to our cultural-ecological well-being to bring our best discriminatory powers to bear upon the sorting out of good and bad apples; not to mistake a mediocre drawing or sculpture or song or poem or story for a good one simply out of loyal affection for its subject matter — Dutch windmills, Chesapeake Bay waterfolk, Parisian boulevards, Polynesian palm trees, whatever.

By way of example, I shall now go out on a loblolly pine limb and maybe step on a few tidewater toes (a good trick when one's out on a limb) by declaring (1) that the youngish writer Christopher Tilghman, for example, whom I mentioned before — of Tilghman's Neck, Maryland, and Harvard, Massachusetts — is an excellent literary artist whose "Maryland" stories (in his collection called *In A Father's Place*, published by Farrar, Straus in 1990) comprise some of the best fiction we have involving the Chesapeake area; and (2) on the other hand, that the late, locally-much-revered Gilbert Byron, formerly of Old House Cove, Maryland (author of *The Lord's Oysters* and other Delmarvania), while a remarkable fellow in many respects, is a (locally) much overrated wordster whose fiction and poetry I cannot imagine any knowledgeable reader taking pleasure in unless that reader's priorities put local folksy subject matter above every other consideration. There are, to be sure, many such special-taste readers (and art collectors): the kind who say, "Give me anything involving the Wild West" — or Labrador retrievers, or sadomasochistic bondage, or what have you, even unto crab-and-oyster harvesters. *Chacun à son goût.*

No doubt there is an inescapable element of personal taste involved in any critical pronouncement such as the one just delivered.* But if we go all the way with "each to his own taste," or call every comparison apples and oranges, we become critically paralyzed; anything then goes, and we can't communicate with one another even for the purposes of reasoned disagreement. This is not the place to draw point-for-point comparisons between the masterful and the mediocre in the work of the two "Chesapeake" writers I've just mentioned — specific instances of perspicacious versus cornball character-drawing, structural craftsmanship, dramatic technique, descriptive precision, verbal texture, thematic depth and the rest. I'll simply put in evidence what I've mentioned in passing already: that Mr. Tilghman's publishers, reviewers and readers tend to be people primarily interested in good writing and only secondarily or incidentally (in many cases not at all) interested in Chesapeake Bay writing, whereas with Mr. Byron the case is prevailingly vice versa — as the overall record of his publishers, reviewers and readership attests.

Enough, however, of that: Gil Byron-bashing is not my concern, except by way of critical illustration. My concern is the aesthetic-ecological argument; that argument may be made with other critical examples than the late laureate of Old House Cove, and from other arts than literature. Let's call Mr. Byron an orange after all, or maybe a ripe Delmarva cantaloupe, and get on with sorting out the apples.

But perhaps the point has been sufficiently made; in any case, I

---

*It may appease Byronistas to know that his most popular tome, the aforecited *The Lord's Oysters*, remains in print partly because I recommended it to the Johns Hopkins University Press some years ago for their "Maryland" series.

prefer to close on a more ecumenical note. Our Chesapeake has many and diverse tributaries, as has its art: major and minor, fair and foul, local and nonlocal, from tiny watershed trickles in Upstate New York and the high Appalachians down to the great ocean itself, when the recycling tide comes in — the Ocean of Story and Panthalassa of all the arts — and including a fair amount of urban runoff and rural manure. Its brackish waters have about the same average salinity as human tears (what writer can resist that datum?), and one side effect of that circumstance is that you can swim in them with your eyes wide open — as I have tried to do allegorically here. On the other hand, those waters are so rich in suspended matter of every imaginable sort, from turds and topsoil to blue crabs and heavy metal, that while swimming wide-eyed through them, you can scarcely see your hand in front of your face.

Caveat natator.

KILLING GEESE

Tom Horton

It is thrilling to watch the flock of wild geese winging confidently on the crest of dawn, closing rapidly the last few hundred yards that separate us. It is rare, when you think about it, for human beings today to see free living creatures that are not running away, shying, freezing in their tracks, programmed long ago to avoid the most deadly species. It's been a trade-off, our becoming lords of earth. In so doing, we have been exiled from the paradise of peaceful coexistence with our fellow creatures, says Konrad Lorenz, the pioneer animal behaviorist who won the Nobel Prize for living with geese in the wild to learn their ways. In those rare moments when wildlings approach us, he says, it is almost as if the exile had been lifted.

Perhaps some notion of this does flicker across our deeper consciousness as the geese sideslip to lose altitude, tumbling like leaves, recovering effortlessly. They swirl down all around us, honking low, soft moans of contentment, feet down, great wings set, cupping the wind, mastering its every caprice and buffet so surely that they seem to descend through some more viscid, stable medium than air. But what we seek so avidly this bright, cold December day is not exactly the paradise of Konrad Lorenz.

"Let's take 'em," murmurs Elmer Crawford, letting fall the goose call he has been blowing so seductively; and the four of us, guns roaring, leap almost in unison from our concealment near the decoys bobbing on the water of the cove.

Even as we rise, the geese have sensed the fatality of their commitment to landing. They struggle to gain altitude, appearing to lumber because they are such big birds; but actually they are gaining about four feet with every wing beat, and I try to lead my targets accordingly. The flock fades quickly from sight, leaving two of its number shattered on the water. Later the dogs will sniff out a third, a cripple, that had glided unnoticed into the marsh during the excitement. By sunset, with another goose and two mallard ducks also in the bag, the hunt will have qualified as a memorable one. Three times we will flirt with the peaceful coexistence paradise of Lorenz and three times we will respond by pulling the trigger.

It seems worth examining whether it must be that way; because when you kill a goose, you have ended something special. Geese, the late Edgar Merkle used to say to me, are smarter than you and I; they mate only once, they protect their children, and they feed their young first. At his Patuxent River farm, Merkle's breeding and conservation efforts through several decades established a flock of more than twenty thousand wild geese on the bay's western shore, where historically there had been none. Why geese? I asked him. He said, "Because I knew the pleasure geese would give people… just to watch 'em, to hear 'em talk just before they take off; just to know they were around. Also they are mostly all Geminis [hatching in May and early June on their Artic breeding grounds], and Gemini is a good sign."

In his convictions, Merkle, who would avidly shoot ducks, but never a goose, was pretty much in agreement with the learned ethologists like Lorenz who have documented the wild goose's extraordinarily close-knit family structure, and a potential for living nearly as long as we (though in the wild it is undoubtedly less). They pair for life, and the loss of a mate can provoke an uncannily human response. "They possess a veritably human capacity for grief," writes Lorenz, who also noted that animals in general, "in terms of emotions…, are much more akin to us than is generally assumed."

I have observed geese that appear to be calling for a lost mate, or a lost flock, and I have no trouble believing they are grieving. In the most ancient parts of the brain, where the deep emotions and instincts are seated, we do not have such different apparatus than a goose. Of course, it is those outsized frontal lobes, sprung forth in just the last few hundred thousand years, that set us apart from the animals. They give us the capacity for rational thought, for choosing between hunting geese and going bird-watching with the Audubon Society, a group, it must be noted, that officially does not oppose hunting. Our big forebrain lets us love geese, even as we love to kill them. That hunting is part of our heritage is as certain as the pointed canines we have in our head, the better to rend meat with. "Man cannot re-enter Nature except by temporarily rehabilitating that part of himself which is still an animal," wrote José Ortega y Gasset, a Spanish philosopher who saw hunting as a necessary, brief escape from the twentieth century. But we are long past those old needs to kill other animals for survival, even to eat meat at all; and so, there we hang, as the geese swirl down to the decoys — civilized hunters, balancing between our canines and our molars, between paradise and exile, faced with a succinct little question posed by the naturalist Joseph Wood Krutch: "Why should anyone kill anything for pleasure?"

Ironically, "the kill" is probably the aspect of hunting that Rooney Crawford, the gunner to my immediate right in the blind, has considered least as a reason for pursuing his sport, which makes him fairly typical of most hunters in the numerous surveys that have been done on what makes them tick. Rooney, forty-one, an affable data-processing engineer from Greenville, South Carolina, has been coming up here every goose season for more than a decade with his older brother, Elmer, fifty-one, a real-estate salesman from Bessemer City, North Carolina. Elmer says he sent away to Maryland for a list of professsional goose-hunting guides and picked Sam Leonard's Friendship Farm, here in Talbot County, by closing his eyes and sticking a dart into the page. The brothers, Rooney says, grew up on a farm in little Clover, South Carolina, hunting squirrel and rabbit as their natural birthright, an easy contact with the land and its crops that he feels society is less and less privy to nowadays.

Rooney says he hunts to be outdoors, for the suspense, for the challenge; and the Crawfords love to eat wild duck and geese. Mostly, though, Rooney hunts for the pleasure of bringing along the fourth member in our blind, his sixteen-year-old son, Mitch. "Mitch began coming here when we had to stand him on a concrete block to shoot over the edge of the blind," Rooney says. There is an easy, joshing camaraderie between the two out here, which reminds me that some of the best times I ever had with my father — some of the best times I ever had — were hunting situations. I don't know that it couldn't have been just as good in other circumstances, but for us it happened on hunts; on kills, if you will.

"The killing," Rooney says with a little uneasiness, but no uncertainty, "it is almost an after-part to the rest… unfortunate, but… " But it has to be there? Yes, it does, he agrees. There is the uncomfortable paradox. Take just about any of the justifications people give for going killing/hunting — being outdoors, obtaining meat, camaraderie — and they all seem things you could experience just as well separately from the hunt. Or maybe not. Up to the time we first shot, the morning had been typical for a hunt at Friendship Farm, which is to say filled with staggering beauty and a senses-swelling awareness of our surroundings. The first fierce blush of dawn kindled cold fires on the smooth surface of Elberts Cove, which edges Sam's farm. The sky was a parfait of creams, pastel blues, palest oranges, and raspberry ices. Increasing daylight developed the landscape like a photographic print as cedars, marshes, and cornfields tugged apart from the featureless grays of night and assumed their own forms, textures, and colors. Crows sallied eastward, cawing. A great blue heron swept silently along the near shore, pursuing solitary routes more ancient, even, than the migrating geese. A swan, big as a ship, sailed fearlessly into our goose decoys, pecking one on the back. We have not hunted its race for centuries, and the swan seemed to know it.

I thought about what Sam Leonard said in the toasty farmhouse kitchen before we walked out to the blind; how he often called his paying customers to give them a chance to back out when he thought the hunting would be poor the next day. They almost never do, Sam said. They just like to be out there… getting a goose is just a bonus. But of all the hunters he has seen, Sam can only recall one who did not go out there at least in anticipation of the kill. He just sat there for three days, never firing his gun, happy as a lark just watching, Sam said. But he was very, very unusual.

Sam doesn't say so, but there is also bonus enough for most of his hunters in spending a day in the blind listening to Sam, or his son, Bobby, who helps out with guiding. Both are as close to natural predators as modern human beings get. They oyster and crab and fish from the waters that edge their farm. They hunt and eat goose, duck, coon, deer, rabbit, quail, dove, and squirrel from the woods and hedgerows that checker their grain fields. I doubt seriously whether they spend a hundred dollars a year on meat from a store. They crop Friendship Farm and its environs in the fullest sense of the word. They know the price of the waterfront land — Sam was offered close to a $1 million for the farm recently; and they also know its value — he turned it down with little thought. Virtually every night of his life between October and March, Bobby, thirty, has gone to sleep to the sound of goose music from the cove by the farmhouse. One Sunday in midwinter, he told me, he had decided to get away, take a drive somewhere. He drove straight to Blackwater National Wildlife Refuge, forty miles away. "I just got the urge to see some geese," he explained.

In the blind, it is nearing noon and nothing much is flying. I have taken advantage of the lull to wander among the decoys and pick up a half-dozen oysters from the clear, elbow-deep water. The water is so icy I have to quit. We open them on the wooden seat of the blind and down them in their cold, salty liquor, with a liberal sprinkling of winter sunlight and clean-smelling air. Good chow, and plucked from nature like that, it somehow satisfies more than just the belly. This is the time of the hunting day to stretch, walk out behind the blind to piss, explore the shoreline, and tramp across a couple fields in hopes of scaring up a rabbit, or quail. Today the noontime entertainment comes from a hawk, whose dazzling power dive undoubtedly translated into death for some hapless creature scurrying frantically through the winter-weary stubble of Sam's cornfield.

"The hawk, the swoop and the hare — all are one," wrote the poet Gary Snyder, in as terse and true an ecological statement as I ever read. The awesome thrill of the swoop, the panic of the cowering prey, beauty and cruel death — each is integral to the very existence of the raptor, and there is not much gain in discussing any part out of context. Suddenly, we are startled by a flash of birds that have moved silently up behind us in the air just off the corner of our sight. I almost spill my mug of coffee. They are only blackbirds, not geese, but it is not unusual for this to happen several times in a day's hunting. Sometimes it is a lone seagull wandering into the periphery of your field of vision; even a sparrow can trigger it.

The reason, I think, is that far from being relaxing, hunting generates a constant and fairly high level of tension, a keen, sense-stretching state in which every subtlety of the tides, wind, weather, lunar cycles, every speck flying on the horizon, becomes worthy of intense scrutiny and endless and pleasurable debate. I have gone birding with expert ornithologists, trekked the Western Maryland mountains with the region's foremost botanists, and pondered the flora and fauna of beaches with noted coastal scientists; but nothing expands my senses to such limits as scanning the horizon, armed, from a goose blind. When seeking to kill, it all matters in a way it doesn't seem to when you are not.

Konrad Lorenz and some others no doubt can extract at least as rich an awareness of nature as any hunter, and on a more intellectual, nonviolent basis; but for the bulk of the 20.6 million Americans who hunt, there may be no fully satisfactory substitute for their sport. As I write, I can hear those who will say that even use of the word *sport* is loading the dice. So yes, "killing for kicks" is also what it is, reduced to its essentials; but surely it is "kicks" that have some pretty complex and not wholly unsavory aspects to commend them. It may be that there are no satisfactory resolutions to the question of killing. Its roots run so deep, are so interlaced with tradition, and evoke so many poignant yesterdays; roots that are too deep to be pulled up and examined, in the opinion of John Madson, a conservation writer.

A national survey by Stephen Kellert of Yale's Forestry School indicates that only about 17 percent of hunters feel compelled to rationalize the deeper urges behind their trigger fingers. I don't wonder. Those are urges for which you can summon some powerful, bloody, and unflattering interpretations: "Men are not friendly, gentle creatures wishing for love," wrote Sigmund Freud, who felt we are motivated by an undeniable, instinctual urge for aggression. He is seconded by the anthropologist Raymond Dart, who believes we have an inbred proclivity for killing, an inherited blood lust, a concept that has been popularized by writers like Robert Ardrey in *The Territorial Imperative* and Desmond Morris in *The Naked Ape*. Certainly I have hunted with people who in their passion for killing come on, as one writer put it, "Like a U-boat commander upping his periscope at Noah's Ark." And I can recall a time, in my teens, when I competed fiercely with a companion in a numbers game to down the most ducks, legal limit and other game laws be damned. I suspect this blood lust, given the nature of teenage boys, is more hormonal than genetic, because it seems a pattern that the need to kill declines in most hunters as they age, though the love of going hunting may never waver. As Chan Rippons, an old Hooper Islander who has quit after slaying more than his share of waterfowl, says, "the older you get, the more you respect life."

At any rate, I prefer the hypothesis of the anthropologist Richard Leakey, who believed that aggression and the hunting instinct are not so interwoven as we had thought. Our capacity to slaughter our own kind in warfare, Leakey thought, is not the product of a hunting society, not the result of something dark and uncontrollable inherited from prehistoric human predators. It is rather a by-product of agriculture. The human economy had to include planted fields and stable settlements as spoils before war became worth the tremendous expenditure of resources it entails. Ultimately, probably all one can certify about our shedding of goose blood today at Friendship Farm is that its motivation lies on a plane above lustful killing and yet surely below Emerson's transcendental communion with the spiritual through nature. To the geese hung behind the blind, it can't make much difference.

Now the sun is almost down. Only the long, red wavelengths of its light linger, stretching across the land, burnishing everything with a warm, coppery glow that belies the fast-falling temperature. Flying so fast they rend the air audibly, six big ducks, creamy undersides luminously rosy in the sunset, wheel across our decoys with a military precision the Blue Angels would envy. Trigger fingers tighten briefly and ease. These are canvasbacks, a protected species since severe habitat loss and hunting pressure devastated their numbers several years ago. "Beautiful, though, aren't they?" says Elmer.

Marsh grass is golden
Under a late sun,
And wild ducks' wings
Whistle with the wind.
We are one,
Wild duck and setting sun.

The young hunter who wrote that half-a-century ago lived just across the Choptank River from Sam's place. Gilbert Byron died in 1991. Renowned poet of the Chesapeake Bay, the poem that contains those lines remained his favorite. He long ago lost the urge to hunt, but the beauty endured, he says. A cuticle of new moon is rising as we pack up geese, guns, and shared memories and head back to Sam's farmhouse, boots breaking thin ice forming in the low spots. Far out on the darkening, slately water a chorus of goose music is piping up that will last all night.

THE STATUE MAN

Robert Day

Long Cove, December 1989

"THEY'RE GOING TO BUILD a statue of me," says Stanley Vansant. Stanley is sitting near a kerosene heater in his marine store at Piney Neck in Long Cove on the Eastern Shore of Maryland. It is the early afternoon of a snowy December day. My wife and I and our friend Kathy Wagner have just brought our boat down river from Scott's Point near Chestertown. We are beginning to thaw out, layer by layer.

Stanley's hardscrabble marina at Long Cove is at the northern end of the Chesapeake Bay. To the northwest about 20 degrees and 20 nautical miles is Baltimore; Annapolis sits to the southwest at roughly the same angle but a few miles closer. Both cities are a short day's cruise by powerboat (a long day under sail), and about two hours by land. Not all that far if what you measure is time and miles. But in terms of culture — and the Eastern Shore culture is what we're going to explore here — it's a lot farther than mere maps can tell.

When we came into Long Cove a little after noon with the snow and tide in our faces, there was a hunter putting out decoys at the shore blind; his dog, a feisty yellow Lab, was leaping out and back at his master's heels and getting tangled in the lines and weights that hold the decoys in place. We could see that the man was yelling at his dog, but we could not hear the quality of his profanity over the noise of our engine. Whatever way he had with the language — and an Eastern

Shore man has some curious turns of phrase — it seemed to do no good against the joy of the dog; as we entered Long Cove, the Lab was retrieving a nicely placed "scout" decoy and taking it toward an inland cornfield.

Now that you are in Long Cove, to get to Stanley's you go all the way to the end, and there you will see that it opens up into a shallow harbor filled with white workboats on moorings or lying up against the piers that jut out from Piney Neck. On the north shore just before the end of Long Cove is a small two-story building rising above the line of sailboat masts and behind an array of Stanley-built workboats gathered there as if they were kids who never left home. Like Harry Truman, Stanley Vansant lives above the store. Stanley is 81. The trip down the Chester River to Long Cove is an annual pilgrimage for us, complete with the recitation of a poem written by Kathy Wagner that celebrates the event. Stanley built our boat — a small sailing bateau made of cypress planking and a pine mast that Stanley and I cut ourselves from the nearby woods. That was a decade or more ago, and ever since then it has seemed proper that when winter comes to the Eastern Shore we should return the boat — still nameless after all these years — to its home.

"When are they going to build this statue?" I ask. Stanley is passing around a faded Polaroid of the plaster cast a Philadelphia sculptor has made. It is Stanley sure enough. He seems to be endlessly tonging for oysters off the edge of one of his workboats. We all nod, but without much enthusiasm; it is not, we think, a good idea to cast Long Cove's aging boat builder in plaster (or bronze for that matter), although we'd rather not say why.

"They won't tell," says Stanley. It is supposed to be a surprise.

About this time Clarence Hicks, a waterman who owns the *Alfred*, an oyster boat named after his son, comes in the shop's back door. The names of watermen's boats on The Shore are not as colorful as the names of the watermen, although you can always tell, by the way, when an outlander from a city suburb has named a boat. Generally it is some abstraction: Wish Fulfilled or My Dream. Sometimes it will have the cuteness of a toy poodle in the back window of a Mercedes: Putt-Putt Heaven or My Present Wife. Watermen tend to name their boats frankly for family.

But if they are plain-speaking in what they call their boats, the names and nicknames they give themselves — or each other — is quite another matter. Paddles Orr, Pickles Munyon, Termite Coleman — and my own favorite, Stump Farney (I think I once ate crabs at the same table with Termite Coleman), and so they have grown large in my imagination. They are famous among the workboats, whoever they are. But as it has turned out, as far as I go with watermen are the likes of Clarence and Stanley.

Clarence was the first waterman to "put up" with Stanley. That was forty years ago. The joke between them now is that they've "put up with each other" all this time. When they play their small verbal game (and they will with pleasure if you lead them into it), they laugh as if it is something newly found: the first crab of summer, the first oyster of winter.

Clarence pulls up a chair, and the five of us take the moment to lean in toward the kerosene heater — an old cylindrical affair that is as blithely dangerous as it is warm. All around us loom the tools and products of boat-yard work: assortments of sandpaper, trowel cement, copper bottom paint, fuel filters, paint scrapers, cardboard boxes of nails and screws (Stanley is a hammer-and-nail boat maker, not a glue-and-screw boat maker), bilge pumps and propellers. Interwoven among the cans of boiled linseed oil and spar varnish are the framed photographs of the boatyard's halcyon days; among them is one of a group of men staring with amusement into the camera lens, and behind them the huge wooden workboat they have built.

"Not much of a surprise," I say, handing Stanley the Polaroid of his would-be statue, "if you already know about it."

"The surprise," says Clarence, who has apparently seen the photograph and is privy to the story, "is where they're going to put this statue. That's what they won't say. I tell Stanley he's going to drive into Rock Hall next summer and see himself big as the bay with all the pigeons in Kent County messing on his head and shoulders right good."

Stanley Vansant leans back away from the kerosene heater, folds his arms across his chest and laughs and laughs. You have to know him to see how he laughs at himself; in the map of his face are all the coves and shoals and inlets of the rough cut lace that is the Eastern Shore.

"That statue will make you famous," I say.

"That's fine," says Stanley, "as long as it doesn't bring me any more business. I got a day's work for every day left in my life."

"I got the same," says Clarence. "As long as the oysters hold out."

"I expect you do," says Stanley. They talk together as if we weren't there.

"A man doesn't need any more work than that," says Clarence.

"Not a local man anyway," says Stanley.

"No, no," says Clarence.

A local man. Two local men in fact. Eastern Shore men. To Stanley and Clarence the land where they live is known simply as "The Shore," and its people are called "Shore folk" or "Shore people," but more often just "locals" — always pronounced with a certain matter-of-factness, as if to suggest by the lack of inflection that no other place could have "locals" and therefore, by implication (an unspoken one to be sure) that the rest of America is probably not much more than roving bands of nomads driving U-Hauls from the suburbs of Washington to the suburbs of Baltimore to the suburbs of Philadelphia. The locals don't need a bumper sticker to tell them there is no life west of the Chesapeake Bay.

On the map, The Shore (always capitalized, as William Warner points out in *Beautiful Swimmers,* "since it is a land unto itself") is an etched strip of rivers and estuaries about 200 miles long running from Back Creek in the northern bay to Adam Island at the southern mouth of the Chesapeake. It is a country composed of part water and part land and part marsh; you get the sense that everything — the people, the language, the customs, the food, the lore — is amphibious. If you stray too far from the bay or any of its estuaries, you are no longer on The Shore, even though you are east of the Chesapeake. Some locals have moved off The Shore by going 20 miles farther inland. If by employing some inexplicable divining rod that, after all, has a limited range, you can no longer sense the tidewaters, you are off The Shore. Too bad. You may be local, but you no longer live where you ought to. Dover, Delaware, is not on The Shore; neither is Rehoboth. Nor is Ocean City, Maryland. Ocean City is especially not on The Shore. But along the Upper Shore — there is a distinction between the Upper and Lower Shore that has to do mainly with the size of mosquitoes and crabs, the larger mosquitoes being to the south and the larger crabs being to the north — Still Pond, Betterton, Fairlee and Chestertown (the jewel of The Shore) are all in "local" country. To the south, Crisfield, Hoopersville, Snow Hill and Cambridge (John Barth country) are all Shore towns.

Some towns — especially in Talbot County — seem about to lose their birthright, not so much because of their geography, but because they have become precious with aging preppies and the Orvis chamois shirt youth set. Easton is something of a model railroad town complete with a local waterfowl festival where you can buy black ducks and canvasbacks forever flying in formation on whiskey tumblers, or paintings of Ralph Lauren-looking chocolate Labradors coming out of the water with unmessed — albeit dead — greater Canada geese.

Just down the road, St. Michaels sports a flashy new hotel on the harbor and a waterman's maritime museum. Where you have museums to watermen you don't have watermen. From St. Michaels in the north to Oxford (Douglass Wallop country) farther south, the shoreline of the creeks and coves is rich with Acorn homes on new development lots or "lovingly restored" 18th- and 19th-century houses on old farms. The oystermen and crabbers in workboats on Plain Dealing Creek maneuver for space against the Hinckley Bermuda 40s and Grand Banks trawlers with their radar turrets whirling away. To the outlanders the locals are quaint — a sure sign of misunderstanding. You may not even be able to find flat ax-beaten biscuits or a good cock fight in Talbot County anymore. In such country the only hope is that the Shore people have gone into hiding while they wait for the BMWs to pass on by.

"Are you local?" I once asked a carpenter building a house in Still Pond. When you want good work done, it's always a question you ask; "good work," mind you, not fast work. The Eastern Shore clock can run in a gifted cosmic slow motion.

"1705," he said.

"I see," I said.

"That's not as local as some," he said, "but it's getting close, now isn't it?"

"It is," I said.

"How about yourself?" he said. He knew the answer.

"Not local," I said.

"I see," he said. He looked at his feet and then at a ragged V of geese passing overhead.

After 20 years of trying on my part — Stanley-built workboat, gunning blinds on the upper Chester, an acquired (and largely fraudulent) bend at my waist as if I'd just come off a morning's tonging or leaning over a trotline, plus a modicum of local phrases I use with aplomb ("that's common" or "I didn't catch the first crab") — I am about as "local" as a cowboy on a camel. In one sense all my efforts to become Shore folk have moved me backward, as if the tide in Long Cove at Stanley's is trying to take me west across the bay where I belong. The main pleasure in not succeeding in my ruse is watching the amusement the Stanley Vansants take in the exploits of foreigners such as myself.

"You picked a good day to be on the water," Stanley says as he takes back his Polaroid. Outside the window of the store the snow is blowing down Long Cove and a crust of ice is edging out from the shores. Stanley's irony is the fulsome kind, complete with a straight-ahead grin. "We heard you were coming," says Clarence.

We thought they had; we had been spotted on the river and we guessed that reports of our madness had preceded us. Both stories and sound travel well over water.

Long Cove, May 1989

We have been working on the boat: painting the bottom, putting in a new bilge pump, sanding the hull, tapping the planks for dry rot. In a few days we'll bolt down the engine and head up the Chester River to Scott's Point at Chestertown for the summer. Sometimes we wonder why we leave Long Cove, but then we remember that part of the pleasure of going is held in the promise we'll return at the end of the season. Usually in cold or snow. One year we got lost and turned around in the fog. Two hours out of Quaker Neck Landing we found ourselves halfway back up the river keeping to the wrong shore going in the wrong direction.

"Have you ever been in New York?" I ask Stanley as we take a break from our work. I think not, and I can't recall now what prompted the question. Maybe the small trip we were about to make; maybe the sense I have that those who have lived on The Shore all their lives have never left it.

"I have," Stanley says. "New York and Europe too. Pearl went with me to New York, and that was enough for her." He is sitting on one of the painted yellow rocking chairs outside his store. There are a few other chairs, and if you work on your boat at Stanley's you are welcome to stop by and sit for a spell and swap stories. Pearl Vansant is Stanley's wife of 41 years.

"I went to Europe by myself," Stanley says.

"What happened in New York," I ask, "that scared Pearl?"

"I got off that train that runs in the ground and she didn't," says Stanley.

"What do you mean 'she didn't'?"

"The train door opened and I got out and she didn't. I could see her crying through the windows as the train went off through the ground."

"What'd you do?" I ask.

"Stayed put," Stanley says. "Pretty soon Pearl comes back. On another train going the other way. Still crying, but this time on the other side of the tracks. That was a mess." He folds his arms across his chest.

"You didn't cross the tracks, did you?" I ask.

"We knew better than that," Stanley says. "But it took longer to figure out how to get back together there in New York than it does to sail out of Long Cove on very little wind."

I think to myself that one day I am going to ask Stanley about his trip to Europe. It's like saving a book by an author you admire.

"I've got to get back scraping," I say.

"You bring your boat down river after the summer?" Stanley asks.

"Yes," I say.

"I'll save you a place," he says.

"Thanks," I say.

"I expect you'll pick a cold day in December," he says.

"We usually do," I say.

"That's true," he says. He shakes his head and laughs.

The Chester River, December 1989

"Where are you heading?" It is the captain of the *Daddy's Girl*, a workboat out of Long Cove, who ties up just one marina down from Stanley's. He is the one who will report that we're coming down the river. There are two other watermen with him; one is at the helm. They have found us just off Quaker Neck Landing. It is snowing and it is going to snow. All down the river (we are about halfway) we have been springing geese into the air; they flock up amid their calling, fly a bit, then circle behind us, filling in the river much as our wake is filled in by the gray water.

Also a small flight of buffleheads has been staying in front of us. They seem to be something of a guide. They take off into the snow, and we lose sight of them until 10 or 15 minutes later when we flush them again. We wonder if they are going to Long Cove as well, or if they will take us up Langford Creek to the north or the Corsica River to the south. In much the same way that we surprise them coming out of the snow and fog, the *Daddy's Girl* has surprised us.

"Long Cove," I say. "We're heading for Long Cove." The captain looks at me with concern; the other men stare. It is as if they have come upon a ship of fools.

And no wonder. To keep warm, my wife (also a Kathy) has dressed herself in two clear plastic trash bags she brought along for more ordinary purposes. She cut a hole in the tops and fashioned herself both a skirt and a poncho. She has reported that this outfit is warm, if not attractive. And who cares — out here on the snowy water in the middle of winter — if it is not exactly Chanel. I tell her to bounce up and down if she wants to get warmer. About the time the *Daddy's Girl* comes upon us out of the snow, she has been bouncing in her plastic bags.

For her part, Kathy Wagner has taken to skipping rope with the anchor line to keep warm. The anchor itself lies stable enough on the floor boards, only its chain rattling. From where I sit, the two Kathys don't seem to have the same beat, so the effect is something like atonal hopping. Sometimes one or the other of them takes to reciting bits and pieces of our boat's poem. Only a man's wife can look lovely to him hopping up and down in the snow dressed in trash bags reciting poetry.

For my part, just before the *Daddy's Girl* arrived I had been sitting on the low bench seat at the back of the boat just behind the engine. To keep my feet warm I'd put them through the hole where the exhaust vents. Every now and then I would get a whiff of burnt rubber when I would get my boots too close. Also, I had been singing. Sound, you understand, carries very well across water.

Dance, dance wherever you may be
I am the Lord of the dance, said He.
And I will lead you all, wherever you may be
And I will lead you all to the dance, said He.

I have a wonderful tenor voice, but I am the only one in the world who has heard me sing who thinks so. Perhaps it is to my bell-like a cappella that the *Daddy's Girl* has been drawn. When I look up and see her large in the fog and snow, I quickly stand, as if in command of my vessel. My wife and Kathy Wagner — who don't see the *Daddy's Girl* — continue to skip and hop. The smell of burnt rubber, I suspect, has carried as far as my singing.

"You sure you're all right?" asks the captain.

They all look at us with the same distant suspicion you see in that George Caleb Bingham painting of fur traders descending the Missouri. Who are these men? Could this be Paddles Orr, Pickles Munyon and Termite Coleman? If so, maybe I am Stump Farney. I have become "local" at last, if madness on the water counts for anything. Everywhere around us the river is white and gray with snow. I realize for the first time that our boat is filling up with it and that instead of testing our bilge pump before we left, I should have brought a snow shovel.

"I think we're fine," I say.

"We can give you a tow," says the captain. One of the men comes up to him and says something in his ear. By now the two Kathys have stopped hopping and skipping.

"No," I say. "We do this on purpose." They stare; the swells of water seem to wash back and forth between us. I want to start singing again, but I don't.

"I expect you do," says the captain after a moment. He nods to the man at the helm, and with a surge of power the *Daddy's Girl* goes off into the snow toward Long Cove. We are left alone to take our nameless boat down river.

Long Cove, December 1989

"Why don't you retire?" I say to Stanley. He laughs. Clarence laughs.

"I did once," Stanley says. "The day I got my first Social Security check I sat in the living room and watched television."

"How'd it turn out?" I say.

"Not much going on," he says.

"What'd you do the next day?" I say.

"I watched it again," he says. "I was common enough to do it twice."

"Then what?" I ask.

"The next day I started building another boat for fear I'd lose the use of myself watching television."

"Would that be our boat?" I ask, trying to figure out the years.

"I've lost track," Stanley says. "Time flies when you're having fun."

We all sit there for a moment, and then I ask him if he'd like us to bring him a copy of the poem we read to ourselves on the water each year when we bring our boat down river. He says that would be fine; he'd like to put it up in the store somewhere. Clarence says maybe it should go on the base of the statue — wherever they put it. I look at Stanley and wonder how impervious to good fortune and fame a man can be. For him I knock on the wood of my chair three times, just under the seat between my legs. He sees me do it, folds his arms and leans back and smiles.

"Have you found a name for your boat?" Stanley says to us. We haven't. Recently we've been thinking of naming it Doctor Leakey, but none of us mentions that. I wonder if that's the test: If we can find, by magic, the right name — The Shore name — for our boat, it will in the quickness of the back-scuttle of a crab make us forever local.

"No," I say. "We haven't."

"Keep looking," Stanley says. "It's here about somewhere." He folds his arms over his chest and laughs.

WATER WARRIORS

Tom Horton

FOR ONE OF THE NATION'S longest running border wars, it seems a lovely and peaceful setting. Another warm, deep summer morning is breaking gently over Chesapeake Bay. The sky has turned from the color of a bruise to dully luminous pewters and pearls. Shades of green, tipped with palest hints of gold, bleed from the dark outlines of the marshes. The rising light urges herons and egrets, also Smith Islanders and Tangiermen, to be about their fishing and crabbing.

A mile to the north, sunrise glints on the white church steeples of Tylerton, southernmost of Smith Island, Maryland's three towns. The village seems a speck afloat on the broad marsh, itself a dot amid the reaches of the mid-Chesapeake. Several miles south, the red blink of a radio tower marks tiny Tangier Island, Virginia. The Eastern Shore mainland, ten miles off, is a smudge in the east, and the western rim of bay across on the Potomac river's mouth is lost in summer haze.

As they have for more than a hundred summers, watermen are slowly and methodically plowing the shallow bottoms here, dragging "scrapes," or toothless dredges behind their boats to capture crabs hidden in the grass beds to shed their shells. From the radios of younger crabbers, the raunchy patter of the "Greaseman," a Washington deejay, blares incongruously. Others are tuned to a gospel station. Suddenly the marine radio channel to which every boat listens crackles a terse message — "Comin'!"

The crabbers, spread across a mile or more of water, react as one. Boats that have been scraping south of Fishing Creek, a small channel that cuts through the lower Smith Island marsh, point immediately northward. A few, well to the south, haul their heavy iron scrapes and leap north under full throttle.

The creek marks the course of the line across the bay that separates Maryland waters from Virginia's. Since it was set in 1632 its location — changed several times — has been a cause for political and legal dispute, gunfire and death. The tradition, now in its fourth century, will continue today.

"In the crick now," the radio warns. All but one boat has made it back into Maryland. A young waterman, "wrung up" fast as he can go, still lacks a few hundred yards of the invisible line. Two bushels full of fat hard crabs, a hard-won morning's harvest, sit on his stern. He can almost taste safe harbor when, buzzing like an angry mosquito, a tiny fiberglass runabout powered by an oversized outboard engine squirts from the marsh creek to head him off.

The waterman has the better angle to make Maryland, but the runabout is far faster. State line and waterman and police boat rapidly converge, and it is the waterman who loses his nerve. Over the stern goes the day's catch, dumped just yards short of the line. The little runabout veers off. He could arrest the waterman, even take his boat in tow to the Virginia mainland miles distant, but the return of the crabs is deemed punishment enough today.

But the little boat is not done. It pulls to a stop directly on the line; and there it will stay, a hateful presence to the crabbers through the long, hot morning, well into the afternoon, until all but a few boats have called it a day.

The marine radio now is alive with conversation, relaying news of the "sneak attack" to watermen up and down the bay:

"Damn that Juney. Somebody oughta' feed 'im to the damn prop [propeller]."

"Baseball bat time for Juney, you ask me."

"Hey, if them oldtime islanders was to come back, Juney 'ud have water from their rifles bustin' in his face… he'd have a reg'lar shower, that he would."

* * *

The object of their affections has a marine radio too, but seldom listens to the watermens' channel. He has heard it all before, and worse. Peter H. Crockett, Jr., "Juney" to the watermen, was born and raised on Tangier Island, where Crocketts were the first settlers in the 1600's. He was the Tangier town policeman until 1978, when he took his present position as a state crab and oyster inspector.

He recalls the first year, 1979, that Virginia assigned him virtually full time to patrolling the line against Smith Island crabbers:

"I was met by eight big workboats, and they got my little 17-footer in a sort of diamond in among them, comin' closer and closer, and I guess they thought they were gonna run me out of the crick. I told 'em the only way they would do that is to kill me. I called in more inspectors on the radio and we arrested the lot of 'em."

Even on his home island of Tangier, Juney says, "I have wrote tickets [for seafood harvesting violations] for my first cousin, for my four brothers… if you can't do that, you might just as well forget this kind of work.

"Now my assistant, when we are home, he almost never goes out of his house; but I go up to the restaurant, get a sandwich… I ain't gonna let anyone keep me in my house. And I won't take nary a free crab or oyster. Damn if anyone feeds Juney, I have told these watermen. If I want a mess of crabs to eat, I'll buy 'em. One thing I have had to give up that I enjoyed was huntin' ducks. It would be too easy for someone to bait my blind [which is illegal] and make trouble."

Several times a summer, Juney will venture, deliberately one suspects, into the lion's den, stopping to have lunch at the stores on Smith Island frequented by crabbers. The mood at such times is no more than strained politeness, and there are times when Juney knows better than to stop in; but it is not uncommon to find a grudging respect for him among some of the crabbers.

"Sometimes he is just outrageous, but he's got a good personality and I guess if he'd gone into politics he'd of been governor of Virginia," says David Laird, one of the island's best softcrabbers: "He'll kick you one second and you'll like him the next."

Over the years the crab cop and the crabbers have sometimes formed love-hate relationships. Juney recalls with genuine fondness one Smith Islander, now deceased:

"He was the type they say around here sorta' changes with the full moon, you know — real friendly one time and a little hell in him the next. Anyhow, he had it in his mind that the true state line run down to Herring Island, which is a few miles below where it is now; and I think the line was set there once [1785] but it hasn't been so for more'n a century.

"Well you know old... once attacked a police boat with a propeller shaft, and one of his brothers tried to chop an inspector's fingers off with a hatchet as he come aboard; and another time I checked him, and he was legal, but he picked up a big mop handle anyhow, and I commenced talkin' real slow to him; I said now..., I have got a .38 special, but that's the last thing we want, for me to have to pull it, now isn't that right... and finally he set his stick down and returned to crabbin'.

"Once, I was a'chasin' him and him in a skiff and he was trying to make for shallow water where my boat couldn't go, and he turned his boat right across mine and I knocked his motor clean off his skiff. Well, I arrested him, and the night before the trial, [he] called and said, Juney, can I get a ride to court? I said sure, and I told him I didn't mean to knock his motor off. He said guilty to all counts, because he wouldn't tell a lie. He was a good man, and I miss havin' him out here."

The law does not always win in such squabbles. One Smith Islander savors the time that "Juney got after me and he could see three bushels of big ole jimmies [male hardcrabs] on my stern, but I got into water that was too shallow for his big Mercury [outboard]. Oh, he druv [drove] 'er til he couldn't drive no further, and I could hear his motor goin' 'eeeer, eeeeeeeer', and I hollered, you ain't gonna make me throw these jimmies over today old Juney. I tell you, he weren't out of heart none [i.e., he was depressed]!"

* * *

The state line that crosses Smith Island, says David Laird, "has been a war as far back as anyone here can remember." A lot farther back than that, in fact. There have been problems ever since the King of England granted Cecil Calvert the Maryland colony in June of 1632. The boundary set across the bay then extended Maryland's jurisdiction up to six miles farther south than it goes now.

Numerous wrangles during the next two and a half centuries set and reset the line's position. For much of that time it was not the water, but the lands on either end of the line that drove these disputes. That changed dramatically in the middle 1800's as the wealth that lay on the bay bottom became apparent.

Between 1839 and 1869, Chesapeake oyster harvests skyrocketed from about 700,000 bushels annually to nine million. The bay was producing nearly half of the world's oysters, a bonanza that eventually would hit 20 million bushels a year in the late 1800's. This period saw the line across the bay turn bloody, with armed conflict and numerous deaths among oystermen and oyster police of both states. In 1877 the line to end all lines finally was set in an arbitration agreed to by both states. Indeed, this line, the same as today's, *looks* designed by committee. Its jagged course, replete with right angle turns, seems strange on the bay's trackless surface; but it reflects the immense embedded wealth of the bottom.

Perhaps the line might have proven satisfactory in a less dynamic environment than that of the bay waterman, whose very survival lies in his ability to be opportunistic, to vary where he works and what he catches. The 1877 line gave Virginia the southern portion of Smith Island, and, at the time, nobody much cared. It was described by the arbitrators as "only a few miles of salt marshes with the exception of four or five acres of firm ground, mere sites for rude fishermen's huts."

Not even worthy of the arbitrators' mention were the thousands of acres of shallow waters within the southern island's marshy boundaries. These were not prime oyster areas, being overgrown with aquatic grasses every summer. But during the ensuing decades, as oystering declined and the crab ascended in value, this bottom would become as valuable to the islanders as the choicest oyster bar, with predictable results.

As if it happened yesterday, residents of Tylerton will tell you about the Evans boy, just a teenager in his first summer of softcrabbing, who was plugged in the back and killed by Virginia police as he sailed his crab skiff below the line.

His grave, in the town cemetery, is dated August, 1900. One old-timer recalls years later at a religious revival asking the boy's father, Captain Mitchell Evans, whether he had come to terms with the tragedy. "It is the hardest thing I've ever had to do," the father reportedly said, "forgive a man for killin' my boy over a crab."

In July of 1926 open warfare broke out in the marshes along Tyler's Creek, a channel leading from Smith Island towards Tangier. A sign erected by Smith Islanders on the bank bore a black hand and the inscription, "we are going to catch swimmers [crabs] or die." In letters to his superiors, a Virginia marine police captain responsible for the area requested extra ammunition and "small cannon or machine guns if possible."

The policeman wrote that "somedays we have had to use two or three boxes of cartridges... to clear the creek for our [Tangier] crabbers"; but the Smith Islanders, firing from impromptu breastworks of water bushes thrown up along the creek, had him outgunned, he complained.

In the late 1940s, a Crisfield crabber, Pete Nelson, was shot fatally in the back by a Virginia marine policeman who boarded his boat just below the line. Calvin Marsh, a former Smith Islander who was crabbing nearby, recalled the scene recently:

"A lot of crab boats closed in on the cop in Pete's boat, and one shouted, 'Let's get 'im', and I think he got scared and that's when he shot Pete with his rifle right in the back. He died before we could get him to Crisfield and had to pour blood out of his boots. I don't think he ever knew what hit him."

* * *

Officially, the 1877 line remains the state line across the Chesapeake Bay, but for a time in the late 1970s, Juney Crockett singlehandedly enforced his own line; and in retrospect, most watermen think he showed more sense than higher officials on either side of the border.

Those were the years of maximum decline in the Chesapeake's underwater grass beds, which had begun to succumb to pollution in the 1960s (they have since come back somewhat, but not nearly to their original condition). Even in the remote and relatively pollution-free crabbing grounds of Tangier Sound, the grasses had declined so that Smith Islanders were pushing farther and farther south into Virginia to find the best softcrabbing.

Inspector Crockett adopted a policy of allowing the Marylanders to venture south to the last point of land on their island, a spot nearly three miles across the literal state line, and not far from the line of 1785, which had been worked out by George Washington and other prominent citizens of Maryland and Virginia.

But pressure mounted for him to enforce the line "right to the foot," Juney recalls. A Virginia marine resources official declared the sanctity of the line to be like the 55 mile an hour speed limit — "it's 55, not 55 and a half."

As Juney and others predicted, strict enforcement led to an historic lawsuit against Virginia by the Smith Islanders. A federal judge in Richmond ruled that just as their quarry — crabs and fish — moves unheeding of political boundaries, so must watermen be allowed to pursue them.

In 1985 Virginia, spurred by the Tangier Islanders, struck back. If they could not keep Smith Islanders from crossing the state line between the two islands, they could pass a law forbidding the keeping of jimmy crabs caught in their softcrab scrapes.

This was a blow to the Smith Islanders. Although the main attraction of the boundary waters is soft crabs, a lucrative sideline is keeping the big, hard jimmies that come there to copulate with the shedding females. For many watermen the extra income from jimmies makes the difference between profit and loss on the season.

Tangiermen say the jimmy crab ban was for conservation reasons, but readily concede that if it keeps the Smith Islanders out of Virginia, well, that is a nice bonus. Unlike the Smith Island scrapers, they catch their hard crabs from the affected area mostly with crab pots, which Virginia allowed to remain legal.

The effect of this has perhaps been less to conserve jimmy crabs than it has made life on the line, in Juney's words, "excitin' almost every day." Few places in either state are carved up now by as many legal lines as these remote and untrammeled marsh and water scapes. In addition to the state line, there are legal lines defining "scrape only" areas, "crab pot only" areas. A crabber can save jimmy crabs in one state, but cannot enter the other with those legally-caught crabs. "Soon we're gonna have to have a lawyer in the stern whenever we go out," Juney says.

* * *

The shame of it is that there probably was a better way, had either Maryland or Virginia ever recognized the fundamental arrogance of attempting to impose fixed lines on a dynamic entity such as Chesapeake Bay. It is the very nature of estuaries like the bay to be restless, a constant battleground between the saltwater of oceans pushing in from their mouths and the sweetwater of rivers flowing seaward, carrying rainfall off the land. In wet years, the rivers predominate and carry hundreds of millions of pounds of extra pollutants from the land; in dry years the ocean's salt progresses miles further up the bay, and the water often clears dramatically.

All this in turn can mean huge fluctuations in where conditions are best for crabbing or fishing, and watermen in places like the Chesapeake have survived by being as mobile and adaptable and changeable as the creatures they catch. In places like Smith Island, every creature, humans and animals alike, must dance to the ebb and flow of tides, the whim of weather and the cadence of the seasons. Nothing is ever static; the only constant is change.

Accordingly, as early as 1949, after the shooting of Pete Nelson, the Crisfield Times in an editorial had urged both states to adopt some sort of floating fisheries zone that would encompass both Smith and Tangier and surrounding fishing communities. It would be jointly managed, but quasi-independent from the fishing rules of either state. Such a scheme has existed for years with the Potomac River Fisheries Commission, and while it is not perfect, it has served to minimize conflict on that river, which serves as the boundary between Maryland and Virginia.

Newspaper accounts from the early 1980s indicate that local crabbers wanted such a solution to avoid filing the federal suit that overturned the state line; but officialdom in both states was adamant. In fact, Maryland even supported Virginia's unsuccessful attempt to hold the line in place.

As both states feared, the lawsuit forced changes that went far beyond the desire of Smith Island crabbers to gain access to a few square miles of grass beds. It has meant that crab dredgers and crab potters from as far away as Baltimore and Rock Hall now flood into Virginia to share in that state's lucrative winter and spring crab harvests. A special joint softcrabbing zone around the squabbling bay islands might still make sense, but for better or worse, the entire Chesapeake is now open to all, and there will be no going back.

* * *

Meanwhile the line, the fixed line across the fluid bay, continues in a dispute that waxes hot with each summer and the coming of crabs to the grass beds of lower Smith Island. Somewhere there is probably a classic picture of just what the islanders think of the line.

In the summer of 1991, Virginia for a time supplemented Juney Crockett's patrols by flying the line in small planes to photograph violators in the act. One day a number of Smith Islanders, as the plane approached, hopped on their engine boxes and all together dropped their trousers, turning hairy behinds skyward in protest.

Juney remains philosophical: "With very few exceptions, they are just tryin' to crab, not bust the law. They got their job and I got mine, and I hope to do it until they carry me off on a stretcher."

THE LINGUIST

Robert Day

WHERE I COME FROM, the High Plains of Kansas, we don't have much water and we don't have any tides at all. Of course, we have tornadoes, as Dorothy and Toto have pretty much told the whole wide world for the last fifty years. The tornadoes have sucked up the water and hauled away the trees. So when I first landed on the Eastern Shore twenty years ago — dropped from my tornado onto the campus of Washington College in Chestertown, Maryland — I was amazed to find the region had both trees and water. Plenty of each.

The trees stayed still, except in big winds, but imagine my surprise when I discovered that the water moved up and down at night. This happened even in the creeks and ponds, which turned out to be not only creeks and ponds but also estuaries and coves and bights — out into which stuck points and necks and peninsulas. When it came to water, especially tidewater, I needed more than a slim dictionary to help me navigate. Not that it wasn't fun to learn the language of my new home; special places require a special language, and you come to know as much about a country — especially this lovely one — through its language as through its geography. It takes both water and words to define the Tidewater.

* * *

"Do you know what a neck is?" I ask. I'm quizzing a friend of mine who owns the Kansas ranch where I used to work. He has "come East" to visit me after all these years, and we are standing at Quaker Neck Landing on the Chester River on the Eastern Shore of Maryland, waiting for the crabbers to return in their bateaux — boats that, I have noted to my friend, are the waterman's version of a cow pony.

My idea is to buy some hard crabs to steam so I can show off my picking skills and teach him some Tidewater words. I have learned quite a bit about picking crabs. I use the "Crisfield-crab-ladies'-method" and have grown accustomed to crabs in all their forms — too accustomed, I realized at lunch the day before, when I ordered a soft-shell crab sandwich.

"Its feet are hanging out over the bread," my rancher friend said. "What kind of sandwich is that when the animal's feet stick out?"

"Soft-shell crab," I said. "Want one?"

He grimaced. "In a steak sandwich — you might recall" he said, "from when you lived in more sensible territory — we take the trouble to trim the beast a bit. No, thank you."

I may have failed to introduce my friend to one of the culinary delights of my adopted country, but perhaps I can still teach him something about its language.

"Don't know what a neck is," he answers my question. "Except in courting."

It's a funny thing about words. When you live in a place for a long time, certain words and phrases seem as natural as the geography.

It's that way in Kansas. "Let's go over to Betty's Tavern in Gorham," my friend might have said to me when I worked for him there, "and have some calf fries with ketchup on them, bolt down a few red ones, grill the county agent about grass tetanus this year — he'll be hanging out doing nothing — and maybe get our fence stretcher back from the town welder." Everybody would have known what we were talking about. They'd even know we'd left our fence stretcher in Hays, not Gorham.

But when you are new to a place, it takes you a while to figure out what is obvious to everyone else. Here on the Eastern Shore of Maryland, not only did the water move up and down at night (and in the daytime, too, I soon realized), but nobody seemed in the least worried about it. And on top of that, they had a word for all this moving water — and for the whole country up and down the middle of the East Coast wherein it moved: tidewater. As in The Tidewater.

Not that folks would go around and ask each other how the tidewater had been doing that year, or if they thought the tidewater would be affected by the price of oil, or if the tidewater had been better in the old days. None of that. It was just that tidewater seemed to have worked its way into just about everything. Like prairie dogs will take over a golf course if you don't watch out.

I learned further that tidewater was not only a word for the way the water moved in this country, it was a word for nearly everything in it: Tidewater Electric, Tidewater Motors, Tidewater Painting Supplies, Tidewater Publishing, Tidewater Funeral Home. Wherever the tide reached — and like a million little fingers it reached way back into the nooks and crannies of the land — there was some enterprise borrowing the name. But that was only the beginning of my new vocabulary.

* * *

We're standing on a neck, I say to my friend as we look downriver to where we can see the bateaux running their trot lines.

"I thought we were standing on a dock," my friend says.

"We are," I say. "A dock on a neck."

In fact we are standing on a pier; the dock — I've learned from those who speak in strict nautical terms — is the water where the boat sits when it is tied to the pier or the wharf (a pier sticks out into the water; a wharf runs along the edge of the water — if you want to get real fancy). Also, I've learned that watermen don't use ropes to tie up their boats; they use lines. I haven't the heart to tell my rancher friend up front that a rope is not a rope, so I think it best to start with the language of geography.

"A neck," I say, "is a thin strip of land surrounded by water."

"How thin?" he says. He looks around. With all the trees growing on it the land looks pretty thick: you can't see any water except the Chester River in front of us.

"I don't know," I say. "But if it gets real thick it's a peninsula."

"I know that," he says.

"But if it's not too thick and it's not too thin, but still a little fat toward the back, it's a point."

"Where's the rest of the water," he asks, "that makes where we are standing a neck?"

"You can't see it from here," I say.

* * *

I know how my friend must feel because when I first poked around on the Eastern Shore I knew the water was thereabouts, but I couldn't seem to find it. The land was flat — just like home — but it had all these trees that got in the way of seeing the edge of the earth. How did you know where you were if you couldn't see the place where it looked like you'd drop clean off? Or how could you know which way was west without seeing the sun melt onto the Colorado line? That being the case, you couldn't possibly know which way it was to water, even though — as it turned out — the water was in any direction you might choose to go.

For myself, I'd learned the best way to find a good stretch of tidewater was to follow a pickup truck towing a boat. Now if you did that in western Kansas, you'd be in Storm Lake, Iowa, at somebody's great-uncle's before you pulled up for the night, but here in Kent County, Maryland, I'd learned that if you followed the right kind of pickup (a rusty and battered one — with bushel baskets in the bed and a battered boat behind — as opposed to an S-10, four-wheel-drive Tahoe), it wouldn't be long before you'd be at some landing or another.

That was another word it took me a while to figure out: landing. All through the Tidewater there are landings. What I couldn't understand was why these driveways into the water — for that is what they are — were called landings. It had an aeronautical ring to it.

Then I realized the word had to be understood from the water and not from the shore. I was landlocked in my thinking. It wasn't the truck I'd followed to Quaker Neck that would do the landing; it was the boat behind the truck—once it came back from crabbing. Of course. When this dawned on me I beat my head with my fist in an attempt to lessen the thickness of my skull. That's when I began to realize that the language of the Tidewater was trying to tell me something: These folks were more rockfish than American bison.

"What will happen if the oysters go bad and you can't tong this year?" I once asked a Rock Hall waterman friend of mine.

"I'll have to go up on land and get a job," he said. To a waterman a job means working for someone else; when you're on the water, you're working for yourself. If you have to go up on land, for sure it's to take a job.

"That's too bad," I said.

"You bet it is," my waterman friend said. "I had an uncle from Hooper's Island who had to go up into the land for a job and he never came back."

"Where'd he go?" I asked. I thought he might say Dover or Baltimore.

"Just up into the land," he said. Since it was off the water, up into the land was all the same to him. Maybe his Hooper's Island uncle made it all the way to western Kansas, I thought; that's up into the land about as far as you can get.

* * *

"We have coves," I say to my rancher friend as I continue my lesson of the day. "And bights and holes and harbors and landings and points and necks and bays and swamps — all right here along this five-mile stretch of the Chester River."

"Do all those places have names?" he asks.

"They do," I say. "Sometimes after somebody. Sometimes after how they look. Piney Neck and Comegey's Bight are both just around the bend. Other names are quite wonderful. Plaindealing Creek. Hilltop Fork. Crab Alley. Bullbegger Creek. Lightning Knot Cove."

"Will a swamp have a name?" he asks.

"Woods Mill Swamp," I say. "In this country they think a good swamp is just as pretty as a good stretch of rattlesnake pasture."

"It's difficult to believe," my friend says. Above all, he likes the rocky beauty of rattlesnake pastures.

"And it's all tidewater," I say. "Swamps and bays alike."

"This river is tidewater?"

"It is," I say.

"What does that mean exactly?" he asks.

"That it flows upstream as well as downstream," I say.

He considers this a minute. "I don't think it's good to stay long in a country where they eat sandwiches with the animal's feet hanging over the edge of the bread and where the rivers run backwards and where" — here he looks around — "you can't see the sun set into the ground."

"You get to like it," I say.

"Maybe," he says. "The water's flat. That's a start."

"They're like us," I say in praise of my adopted country. "Only different."

"Somebody told me before I left," he says, "that a rope isn't a rope on the water."

"You're learning," I say.

"You come home," my rancher friend says, "to where folks put ketchup on their calf fries and the creeks run the right way."

"I will," I say. "But I'll live here, as well."

* * *

It's a pleasure in life to have two homes if what you mean by that is two ways of talking. But even after twenty years, it still amazes me that the tidewater down at Still Pond Creek — not far from where I live — isn't "still" at all but is rising even as I am writing these words, and in so doing is flooding the marsh grasses and filling up the coves and creeks and bights and forks and swamps all up and down the Chesapeake Bay — and even farther south than that. And everywhere it flows into the country, the tidewater is laying claim to its name.

"What's a calf fry?" my waterman friend asked me one day when he learned I was from the west.

"A prairie oyster," I said.

"You tong them on the bars or along the edge of the channels?" he asked.

"It is not like that," I said. "There's no water in my country."

"You got oysters and no water," he said. "Some things are difficult enough to believe without you telling stories."

Maybe one day I'll introduce my waterman friend to my rancher friend and kick back and listen to them swap lies: red ones, snooks, gomer bulls and peelers. I wonder what knot you use to tie ropes to lines, and how far the prairie can stretch and how deep into the country the tidewater can flow.

A VIEW FROM THE NORTHERN NECK

Eugene J. McCarthy

RAPPAHANNOCK COUNTY has not changed very much since I first wrote about it five years ago. It is still seventy-five miles and seventy-five years away from Washington, D.C. The ruins of old mills still mark the courses of small rivers, runs, and creeks. The number of churches, roughly fifty, serving slightly more than 5,000 persons, or souls (one church to 100), is about what it was five years ago. A few church buildings have been given over to other than religious purposes, in a way reborn or reincarnated. Neither word quite applies. In one case, an Episcopal church in Sperryville has been deconsecrated and is now a craft shop, which would seem to be, if a church had to go, a good way to go. The number of post offices at last count is still nine, approximately one for every 500 persons, or one post office for every ten churches. There is, as was the case five years ago, no drug store and no liquor store in the county and nothing that could be called a supermarket or a shopping mall. Population growth has been minimal, close to zero, and the Gross County Product, the local equivalent of the Gross National Product, has been stable, that is, somewhat short of the reported national level. The sub- or secret-economic statistics for the county have never been firmly established. A cursory survey indicated that, as previously, most residents of the county, in the event of a nuclear war would rather see or meet Carrol Jenkins approaching with his pick-up truck, chain saw, and other equipment, than the President of the United Sates in a helicopter or the Secretary of Defense in an M1 tank.

Reverend Jenks Hobson remains the most trusted clergyman of the county, as attested to by the fact that he still is asked to bless the hounds at the opening of the Fall Hunt. He has been asked why, in the course of his blessing the day before the hunt, which includes the riders, the horses, the hounds, and the fox or foxes, he does not include the chickens that are scattered along the prospective route of the ride. Buster Hitt is looked upon as the person most to be trusted if you are interested in used cars, and Junior Baldwin, if you live in the western part of the county, as the best repairman, far superior to Mr. Goodwrench or the Midas man. The groundhog remains the most despised and hated animal in the county, especially by James Kilpatrick, nationally known columnist and a great nature lover, who, it is reported, remains hopeful that a scroll may be found in some high Judean cave establishing the Biblical curse that mentions thorns and thistles also included groundhogs, thereby giving him scriptural support for his natural case against that animal.

The heavy discussions of national and international problems take place three or four times a week during the lunch period at the Corner Post Restaurant in Flint Hill. More immediate, and possibly more pressing problems are dealt with in the early morning gatherings at the W. and J. store on Route 231 beyond Sperryville, a store noted as the "last stop" (depending on what you may be stopping for) before Old Rag Mountain.

Actually, what takes place is not so much a gathering as a kind of moving or fluid discussion in which the participants come and go. In the course of the hour and a half from seven-thirty to nine o'clock, on any morning of the week, participants in the discussions may include woodcutters and wood haulers, horse and mule traders, a rattle snake hunter, a game warden, a sheriff's deputy, a photographer, orchard men, lawyers, haymakers, and others. The military is represented principally by colonels, although occasionally, in the absence of the established colonels, someone will acknowledge that he was something less than a colonel. The whole proceeding is managed by Wilma Burke who runs the store. Not all stores in Rappahannock County are owned or run by Burkes, but it seems to be better, if one is in the store-keeping profession, to be a Burke or to be married to one. Consumer protection is taken care of at W. and J.'s principally by anticipation of trouble, preventative action. The banana, occasionally offered for sale, is the only fresh fruit ever available, and the tomato, the only fresh vegetable. The staple offerings in the fresh or natural order are potatoes and standard onions of good size and not of any of the varieties that are advertised as not causing eyes to water, or as tasting like apples.

The store itself, at least in the morning hours, is kind of a sanctuary. Privacy is respected. Any exaggeration is tolerated and allowed, even encouraged, unless it downgrades the character of some person. There are no limits on what may be told, of war, of coon hounds, of fox hounds or of beagles, of game sightings and success in hunting. I have reported having seen as many as thirty wild turkeys in a flock, three bears and three bob-cats without noting any raised eyebrows. Reports on mountain lions are more suspect, only one sighting claimed by John Glasker having gone unchallenged. Reports of success in betting on the horses at the Charles Town track are definitely suspect.

The highway department continues its three times a year attacks on roadside wild flowers: the first when the white daisies are in bloom, with supporting blue chicory; the second when the day lilies flourish, and tickseed and yellow daisies; and the third when chicory, wild sunflower, buttonweed and butterfly weed take over. The highway department also disrupts traffic, building three-lane bridges on two lane roads and leaving the one lane bridges on two lane roads. Larry LeHew, the well digger from Front Royal, is still revered for having dug the well that provides just the right volume of water for Washington, the county seat; just enough to meet the needs of thirst and sewage, but not enough to encourage growth or waste. Larry is looked upon as a kind of Moses who brought water out of rock but without subsequently imposing commandments.

Cemeteries: Plastic Roses in the Snow

It cannot be said of Rappahannock County, as can be said of the earth, that there are now more persons living on it than have lived on it during all of its previous existence. There are more persons who have lived in Rappahannock County, died, and been buried here than there are in the current population. Cemeteries are given serious attention in the county. Adjacent to most older houses, or marking where such houses once stood, are small cemeteries, some still well maintained, enclosed within stone walls, some with rail fences, and some with wire. Some have been kept free and clear of trees. Some are overgrown and marked by thickets of sumac, of locust, of sassafras, or hemlock. A few are marked by ancient oaks and cedars. Of later age and varying condition are cemeteries adjacent to old churches with graves marked by weather-worn limestone markers, some in their leaning defying gravity. Names and dates of birth and death are still legible on some, but faded beyond perception on others. In churches still active, at least for burials, granite markers stand among or adjacent to the limestone and marble. Graveyards remain in use, even when churches are closed or gone, like that of the Episcopal Church in Woodville that was destroyed by a tornado years ago and never rebuilt. It seems to be an ecumenical cemetery, possibly accepting the remains of Catholic dead who otherwise might be buried in Culpeper, or in other Catholic burying grounds, or in military cemeteries if they qualify for military burial.

There are community burial grounds, most notably in Flint Hill and Sperryville. Flint Hill bans the placing of plastic flowers, except from November 1 to March 31. Sperryville has no such limitations, and plastic shows on that hillside place in all seasons — plastic roses in the snow of December, unfading daffodils in the autumn, and again, against the green of spring, mixed with flowers brought from garden and from pot. Easter lilies that will stay on, unchanged, until September, and occasionally the quiet, unchanging peace is marked by a spinning sunflower turning on its wooden stem. Then again, late in the year, come the plastic roses in the snow to show the men who roll the eighteen-wheelers down Route 522 that someone remembers and is true.

Fences: From Robert Frost to Paul Mellon

Fences come in a great variety of materials, form and purpose. Good fences may not be quite enough to make good neighbors here, as Robert Frost said they do, or did, in Vermont and New Hampshire. But bad fences, here, certainly make neighbors unhappy. This is especially true if a bull gets through one to heifers not yet ready to be bred, or an unregistered bull intrudes upon a herd of pure-bred cows.

The most respected fence in the county is stone, full height, standing without help of mortar, unaided by boards, posts, or wire. It tells of hard work in clearing fields of rock, of careful building and rebuilding over many years.

Not far below in rank is the half-stone fence, topped by a rail supported by crossed posts or by a post-supported board or two, possibly fortified by hidden wire and with a strand of barbed wire allowed along the top. These are known as "Middleburg" fences or Mellon or Rockefeller fences.

Next in generic ranking of fences are those of wood: of rails, and boards, and wooden posts. In this class the species ranked first is the worm fence, with oak rails, supported by crossed posts, mainly of oak, not sunk in the ground. These are now largely ornamental or ceremonial, marking the lines and limits of old battle fields. A new form of worm fence invented recently by Donnie Keyser, a neighbor, is made of mountain locust rails, laid rail on rail, six deep with crossing ends, and nailed with spikes when not yet dry, six rails in height and sure to last a lifetime.

The most common rail fence, and most used, is the "two post" fence laid in straight lines, and two posts, at measured intervals, bound with wire, sustaining oak rails, some new cut, but most reborn from an earlier fence life. The posts may be of locust or of treated woods, and the rails aided by a strand or two of barbed wire.

One may see occasionally a fence with rails or poles cut and set in holes in posts, but such fences need not be taken seriously by fence watchers, as usually they enclose no more than grass, and trees, and shrubs, and people.

Board fences are fairly standardized as to material, purpose, and style, with slight variations. They are practical fences used for yards, small plots and pens, and pastures. They serve well for horses, and for all breeds of cattle. The posts are usually split locust or treated cedar, the boards of oak, nailed in orders of three or four to the posts. Some fence builders choose to nail the boards on the inside of the posts, a reasonable choice since cattle push from that side. Others nail the boards on the outside of the posts, and some cover the joined boards with a board running vertically at each post, for strength and also for appearance's sake. Practical fence men say there is no good reason for this way of building fences.

A few board fences usually of short length, are painted white, but most are treated, sprayed, or painted, showing black. Some fencers, cattlemen, not concerned with appearance but with service, and not raising cattle to outdo the income tax collector, leave both oak and locust unpainted, letting nature have its way.

The third group of fences given place and recognition are of wire — at the lowest level simple barbed — with as many as four strands, generally frowned upon except as supplemental to other fences, but tolerated in what may qualify as a temporary fence (not quite as temporary as a single strand electrified fence) around a field in soil bank or a hayfield or an orchard for post-season grazing. The wire fence most commonly used by those who practice some form of agriculture or livestock raising or feeding, for a livelihood if not for profit, is a basic fence of woven wire topped by one or two strands of barbed wire, sustained by posts of varying kind, with locust or cedar as a rule, sometimes with lesser posts of steel or spindly locust set between the heavier posts. Such fences are all-purpose. They will hold horses, cows, sheep, and even swine. Some fence builders prefer a narrow roll of woven wire with space below it for one strand of barbed wire, the easier to do battle with honeysuckle, the major enemy of fences in the county.

And then there is the prince of woven wire fences, for horse farms, of the highest order, triangularly woven, guaranteed proof against any horse's folly, and with one board at the top to protect the head and neck of thoroughbreds.

There is one other fence of late introduction, unproved and therefore not generally approved: a high-tension fence with smooth wire running free in staples or eyes, infrequent solid posts, with spreaders in between and provision for electric help, to hold disrespectful cows.

Beyond the accepted posts, and strands, and boards, and rails, are the fences of the shiftless: a mixed lot, somewhat like the cattle they attempt to hold: parts of old stone fences, or of old rail fences, with interweaving of woven or barbed wire, fastened to whatever is available, downed trees and standing ones, steel posts, pipes, parts of iron beds. Fences, local experts say, can, if you study them carefully, tell a lot about the character of farm owners, their wives, their economic status (real or desired, improving or declining), major sources of income, kind and value of horses or cattle being pastured, regard or disregard for neighbors, for wildlife, especially for quail, for nature (honeysuckle, trumpet vine, brambles, dogwood, hawthorn, or any combination of the above). A board fence, with faded and flaked paint and some broken boards, usually indicates that the farm or its owner once knew better days. A pasture with economically and socially more acceptable fencing, say rail or board, on the front or road-facing line, and lesser fencing on side or back sides, indicates concern for social acceptance rather than concern for economic realities. Farms with extended board fences enclosing a whole pasture of some size are usually marked as being supported, directly or indirectly, immediately or remotely, by revenue derived from sources other than the current farming operation, either inheritance or income tax avoidance. Character and social aspirations of wives, too, can be read into quality of the fences and into painting and treatment of fencing. Fences broken down and loaded with honeysuckle are usually read as signs of surrender whereas those with hedge roses and brambles may indicate a friendship for quail. Some experts can easily tell, they claim, what kind of cattle the fence was built for (or what kind of horses and sheep). They also distinguish among breeds of cattle, Angus requiring the tightest fence. Nothing in the county is ever quite as simple as it seems.

The Guns of June and July: Groundhog Days

In three years of residence in Rappahannock County, I found that persons living in the county, and especially those living in the area of Scrabble and Hawlin Hollow, had a deep respect and love for all animals, both domestic and wild.

They were not overly sentimental. They acknowledged the laws of nature, accepting that hawks would prey on field mice and on lesser birds; that foxes would eat moles and rabbits and occasionally a chicken; that raccoons would eat frogs, birds' eggs, and other things; that skunks had a right to life, along with opossum, chipmunks, and squirrels.

They would use animals against animals in civilized ways: fox hounds to chase the fox, coon hounds to pursue the wily raccoon. They rode horses. They hunted deer, quail, wild turkey — even bears — in season. Poachers were not socially approved.

Among all of these considerate and animal-loving people, three were outstanding: one, a journalist, writer, especially partial to collies of any size or color but to all other animals, I thought, understanding and friendly. He had written a book about the wonders of animals and maintained the best bird feeders in the county.

The second was a semi-retired professor, a gentle person, a lover of animals. He fed birds and chipmunks, put salt out for deer, maintained oak trees for squirrels and even an old, hollow, unsightly basswood tree for bees.

The third was an airplane pilot, sustained in his love of animals by his wife. Together they kept three Golden Retrievers who retrieved only tennis balls and Frisbees. They supported two horses, which they never rode. They had a tom cat, blind in one eye, who spent one third of his time in the veterinary hospital, one third of his time away from home, and one third of his time patrolling the house, holding the mice at bay as his mistress refused to use traps or poison. They had for a time four geese. When two of them disappeared just before Christmas and two at Easter time, rather than believe the obvious that the geese had been taken by foxes, leaving no trace of feathers, they accused two of their most trustworthy neighbors of having stolen the geese.

Thus man and nature seemed in perfect harmony in Hawlin Hollow and Scrabble, until one night at the journalist's house when the talk turned to dogs. I entered the conversation, speaking for my Australian Shepherd. She had not proved herself in handling sheep or cattle, I admitted, but she did have a potent herding instinct and was most gentle with animals.

"Only yesterday evening," I reported innocently, "I heard her barking in the yard. I went out to see her herding a young groundhog very carefully until it climbed into the lower branches of a small magnolia tree. At which point the dog, apparently believing she had accomplished her mission, abandoned the groundhog in the tree."

I stopped, waiting for approval. None came. There was a pause, then the journalist asked in what I considered a suspicious tone, "What did you do with the groundhog?"

"Well," I said, "I put the dog in the house, took a broom, poked the animal out of the tree, and chased it off into the woods."

There was a shocked silence. Neighbor looked at neighbor. I was puzzled. I asked myself had I offended someone or someone's dog, or abused a groundhog?

In Minnesota, my home state, groundhogs are of minimal interest and are seldom mentioned excepting as weather prophets on or about February 2nd. I recalled having seen dead groundhogs, tied by their tails, hanging from the branches of trees along country roads in Rappahannock County. I waited in a state of mild apprehension.

The author of the animal-loving book finally broke silence.

"You let the goundhog get away!" he exclaimed. "Why didn't you kill it?"

"I don't have a gun," I responded.

"Then why didn't you use a club? Do you know what you have let loose in this county?" he continued. "That one groundhog in its lifetime can dig enough holes in pastures and in fields to cause ten or fifteen horses to fall and break their legs. Riders will be crippled, possibly killed. That one groundhog and its progeny will destroy hundreds of pounds of garden crops and acres of sweet corn."

"You," he concluded, "had a groundhog treed and let it go, when I spend days lying in wait for one to show up near my garden."

"Groundhogs," he added, and he is a religious man, "should never have been allowed on the Ark."

I left the party early.

The next morning, as I was driving into town to pick up my mail, I approached the house of the college professor. As I neared the house I saw the gentle professor, or so I thought to be, coming down the road. He was wearing a baseball cap, his usual attire for his daily walk. But today he was not walking. He was moving in a stalking crouch, and carrying a rifle.

I slowed to a stop as I reached him. "What's wrong, professor?" I asked.

He looked up at me from his crouched position. His eyes were bright with a light I had never seen in them before. "Groundhog," he hissed. "Keep going."

I went on and got my mail. On my return I stopped to see how the professor was. He had returned from the hunt and was sitting quietly on his front porch drinking lemonade. The strange light had gone out of his eyes. I ventured to ask him about the groundhog. "Dead," he said. "I got him with one shot." He then went on to tell me that in his lifetime he had killed more than one hundred groundhogs, and that he hoped to increase the number greatly now that he had more time.

Later in that same week, on an afternoon walk, I stopped to visit the airline pilot and his wife. On being admitted to the kitchen, the first thing I noticed was a 30-30 rifle leaning against the kitchen stove.

I had never seen a gun in the house before.

"What's the gun for?" I asked.

"What for?" the pilot responded. "What else but for shooting groundhogs?"

"Your wife won't let you shoot them, will she?" I asked. I had seen her cry when the pigs were slaughtered in the early spring.

"She loads the gun," her husband replied.

I called my gentle dog up from under the table, got safely through the three Golden Retrievers that were guarding the kitchen door, and headed for home.

As I walked down the lane, I could hear behind me the sound of gunfire echoing through the hollow.

Mollie: R.I.P.

My dog "Mollie" spent the best days of her life in Rappahannock County; irregularly, a few days or a week at a time between her second and fourth years; and then with a permanent address and residence, interrupted by days and weeks in Washington, D.C. until her death in 1988. It was here that she learned what ice is, and groundhogs and bees; met skunks and 'possum and raccoons; sensed the presence of bobcat and bear; and practiced her herding skills whenever given a chance with children or cows. Once kicked by a horse she gave up on horses; outsped by rabbits and deer, she ignored them. After one experience with an electric fence, she would enter pastures only through open gates.

She learned respect for cats, but not for dogs, nor for people who laughed too loudly or waved their arms without purpose or shuffled their feet beneath a table.

Mollie was an Australian Shepherd. Australian Shepherds are an unusual breed first recognized and registered in the United States some thirty years ago. The breed, or what became "the Breed," was brought here from Australia (where it is believed it picked up some "Dingo" blood) by Basque sheepherders. The dog is mainly of Spanish origin, although there is a school of dog experts, a very limited one, that holds that some of the dog's ancestors were Celtic.

In any case, the Australian Shepherd is no ordinary dog. It is, my dog book states, distinguished by "character and intelligence," rather than color, size or conformation. Its eye colors can be blue, brown, hazel, amber, or any combination, with no order of preference. Mollie had one brown eye and one blue one, the combination I prefer. Her ears were as they should be, not pricked or hanging, but broken about three quarters from the base, indicating a restrained alertness. She was "blue merle." Some Australian Shepherds are born with a natural bobtail. Some have to be docked. Mollie, the record states, was docked.

Australian Shepherd owners (that word must be used with qualification, since an Australian Shepherd can never be wholly owned in the way that most other dogs can be, with accompanying obedience, even subservience) are resigned to the difficulties of showing their dogs. The problem exists at the lower levels of canine competition, the level at which the "best of breed" is determined. Every Australian Shepherd, unlike Australian Cattle dogs, or other breeds such as Beagles and Golden Retrievers, is different from every other Australian Shepherd. Each in its own way, therefore, is "best of breed." An Australian Shepherd owner never has to apologize or defensively admit any deficiency in his or her dog. Owners of Golden Retrievers are quick to say, even without challenge, that their dog's nose is a little too long, or that its color is a little off, or that the dog's hind quarters are not quite right, etc. Somehow, by lot possibly, if an Australian Shepherd could get through the barrier within its own breed and be entered in the contest "best of show," any Australian Shepherd could win.

Meanwhile the Australian Shepherd waits, remaining true to itself — and resisting the corruption of cross-breeding. One sled dog owner thought that by crossing a sled dog with the Australian Shepherd, noted for its intelligence and endurance, he could develop a super sled dog. His experiment did not work. Australian Shepherds are not meant to pull loads. Even when bred down to one quarter Australian Shepherd, the dogs, although they would keep the traces of the harness taut, would not pull.

Their herding quality, the experimenter reported, remained unchanged and when released at the end of a sled run, they would occasionally herd a moose into camp.

Mollie is gone.

Mollie

I know that you will not come back,
Not answer to my call or whistle,
Not come even at your pleasure,
As was your way.
Yet, I will leave your "good dog" pad and dish
Beside the kitchen sink, a while,
Your rawhide bone beneath a chair,
The cans of dog food on the shelf,
Your favorite ball,
Hid in the boxwood hedge.
I'll listen in the early morning light,
For your muted huff, not quite a bark,
Suggesting you be let out.
And lie in half-sleep until
I hear your harp-like,
Single scratch upon the screen,
To signal you had answered nature's call,
Made your accustomed rounds,
Checked the limits of the grounds,

For trace of groundhogs, raccoons, even bears,
And now returned intent on sleep
On bed, or rug, or floor,
Depending on your mood.
And if not answered,
Lie down in silent protest
Against my failure to respond
And to show resentment of the
Indifference of the stolid door.
I will not yet remove
The mist of dog hair
From your favorite chair.
Not yet discard the frazzled frisbee
You could catch, making plays,
Going away, like Willie Mays,
But having proved your skill,
Refused to fetch.
Let retrievers tire themselves
In repetitious runs, you seemed to say.
You would run figure eights,
Disdaining simple circles,
Jump hedges just for sport.
Eat holes in woolen blankets
But leave untouched
The silk or satin bindings.
Herd sheep and cattle,
Spurn running rabbits and deer,
That would not play your game.
You swam with ducks
And walked among wild geese,
Ate Tums but not Rolaids.
You knew no dog-like shame.
And died by no dog's disease at end,
But by one that also lays its claim on men.

PITCHING

Robert Day

"SEE THAT GRAVEYARD over there?" says Ed Athey, athletic director of Washington College and head coach of the school's baseball team. We are standing on the pitching mound of Kibler Field in Chestertown Maryland. This is more than twenty years ago.

"Yes," I say. The graveyard toward which Ed is pointing shelves itself on a hill behind the third base dugout and beyond the railroad tracks of the local grain train that cut through the back of the college campus. It is out of reach of even the greatest slugger's drive: Not Swish Nicholson, not Home Run Baker, not even Jimmy Foxx in his prime could have hit a pitch into the Chestertown graveyard from where Ed and I are standing.

"What about it?" I say.

I am Ed Athey's new pitching coach, a volunteer from the faculty who has a modest career in high school and college to his credit.

For the previous hour or so I have tried to realize ("revitalize" is the word I really see in my mind's eye, but I am keeping that to myself) my baseball youth by hurling batting practice to the lean and hungry hitters of the Washington College squad. It has been slow going. My old form is no doubt somewhere in the arrangement of the bones and muscle and cartilage of my burgeoning middle-aged body, but an afternoon of throwing has not yet brought all these parts into anything like the dependable prose rhythm you need to pitch well.

Two pitches in point: My curveball (which out of vanity — and, I have noticed, to the barely contained amusement of the young hitters — I signal with a twist of the wrist before I throw so the catcher and batter know what's coming) has more the droop of a chewed toothpick than the fishhook it needs to fool keen eyes. Eddie Lopat (who had three speeds of curveball: slow, slower and slowest) is Bullet Bob Feller compared with me this afternoon. And my fastball—which even in my youth was never anything to point a radar gun at—seems to have lost what movement it once had, unless you count as "movement" a decided dropping off at about sixty feet-six inches as if, approaching the end of a long day, it wanted to plop itself down on a couch for a nap.

Beyond these two staples in my repertoire I have tried my Hoyt Wilhelm knuckleball (in the dirt five out of five times, although one hitter hit it on the bounce for a clean single to right); my Ewell Blackwell sidearm cross-fire (thrown about a foot behind a startled right-handed hitter two out of two times); my change-up (telegraphed so clearly that it looked more like Satchel Paige's "hesitation" pitch: two blows, both out of the park); a Christy Mathewson "fadeaway," the ancient version of a "screwball" (hit over the left field fence two out of five times); two sliders (no slide, no drop, nada: deep hits); two spitballs (one resulting in a clothesline drive down the third base line and one in a rifle shot back through the box that made me feel like Herb Score when Gil McDougald took aim); and finally some Walter "Big Train" Johnson semi-submarine pitches, most of which hit high on the backstop and dropped to the ground like dead pigeons. In this version of my "revitalization" I begin to see myself as some slow-pitch softball moundsman sent onto the field by Bill Veeck to bring comic relief to an otherwise dull game: Call me Eddie Gaedel. Ah, the stages of life.

"There are arms in that graveyard," says Coach Athey, giving me a wan smile and a pat on the back because Ed can no more be cross with a man than he can tell a story that isn't true, "there are arms in that graveyard that have more life left in them than yours."

Truth is a fastball high and tight that backs you out of the box every time.

The Eastern Shore League, Then and Now

The Eastern Shore of Maryland was once wonderful baseball country. If you believe in ghosts, as in the real live Ed Athey — who retired as athletic director a few years back but still coaches the Washington College team — it still is. The truth of my dead arm is another matter.

From about 1922 until 1949, the towns that sprawl along or near the coves and creeks and estuaries on this side of Chesapeake Bay fielded a number of Class D minor league teams. In Maryland, Crisfield and Salisbury and Cambridge and Easton and Pocomoke City all had teams at one time or another. In Virginia, teams represented Parksley and Northampton County; while in Delaware, Dover and Laurel among others, they put players destined for the major league onto the field. "Shore hopes," I believe these players considered themselves. And Shore hopes might well have been what they thought they were cheering.

Most of the ballplayers on these teams were not home-grown. They shagged flies and fielded grounders and doubled to left among the soybean fields and the peach groves and the cantaloupe patches long enough to ripen for the big leagues: strangers in the land of pleasant living. Mickey Cochrane (Athletics and Tigers, catcher), Joe Collins (Yankees, first baseman), Carl "The Reading Rifle" Furillo (Dodgers, outfielder), Danny Murtaugh (Pirates, second base and manager), Red Ruffing (Red Sox, Yankees, pitcher), George "Twinkletoes" Selkirk (Yankees, outfielder) and Mickey Vernon (Senators, first baseman) all once saw action on the Eastern Shore. At least two major league umpires (Larry Napp and Frank Dascoli) called balls and strikes in such towns as Centreville, Maryland, and Milford, Delaware. Connie Mack himself once served as president of the Federalsburg A's. But most of the Eastern Shore League's national fame comes from strictly local heroes.

Driving into Sudlersville, Maryland, from Church Hill, Maryland, along Route 300, you cross Dell Foxx Road. Note the two x's in Foxx, the same two employed by James Emory "Double X" Foxx, the author of 534 career home runs and a .325 lifetime batting average. Dell Foxx — or Mr. Dell, as he was called — was Jimmy Foxx's father. While Dell Foxx Road is a memorial to the farm family that reared the great Athletic and Red Sox driver, a large engraved stone in the center of Sudlersville is the town's tribute to the hitter himself.

Not far away in Chestertown, near the town hall, is a statue in honor of Bill "Swish" Nicholson (all-star outfielder for the Cubs and still very much alive, thank you), his bat finishing a swing that has no doubt hit one clear into the Chester River, three blocks away. The nickname, by the way, came from what Ed Athey calls the "emphatic" swing Nicholson had.

"If he missed a pitch, you could hear his bat cutting the air," says Ed. "When he came up to the plate the fans would cheer, 'Swish, Swish, Swish.' It would go around the stands like a wave."

As for Frank "Home Run" Baker of Trappe, Maryland, he got his name when — as a third baseman for Connie Mack's Philadelphia Athletics — he pounded a game-tying homer against Christy Mathewson (the Prince of Pitchers) of John McGraw's New York Giants. It was in the third game of the 1911 World Series, and while Home Run Baker led the National League that season and the three seasons after that, he did so — in that pre-Ruthian era — by hitting a dozen or fewer home runs a year.

The Radio, Circa 1950

By stringing a few extension cords together I could get my father's basement radio (a pre-portable model) halfway down the gravel driveway that abutted the dirt road that ran by our house. On the other side of the road were a vacant yard to the northwest (right field) and an abandoned house to the southwest (left field). Deep center (due west) was the remains of a back yard picket fence. Home plate was the end of our driveway. Balls were rocks from the driveway, while my bats were a series of "hitting sticks" I would fashion out of scrap from Father's carpentry projects. The ballgame itself (in which I was always the batter) would be dictated by the Saturday or Sunday afternoon radio broadcast of the out-of-town games played by the Kansas City Blues, a Triple-A farm team for the New York Yankees. Although the three-person Day family lived deep into the country west of Kansas City, I was — as it turned out — not a boy too far from town to learn baseball.

Cerv hits a drive deep to left — back, back, back. It is going. It is going. It's gone. It is over the fence. A two-run homer for Bob Cerv with Bill Renna scoring in front of him. What a drive, folks. What a drive. Out of sight.

As Bill Renna had already singled sharply to center with a rock shot over the road and into the grass just beyond the drainage ditch, it was only a matter of putting Bob Cerv's homer over the roof of the vacant house (on the roof was a triple; against the wall was a double), something I could usually do before the next batter came up, but not without a few foul balls and a couple of grounders that didn't count in the game of my dreams. Sooner or later there would be that solid whack of my hitting stick against a good round rock, and off Cerv's drive would go in perfect imitation of what happened on the radio.

What my father thought of all this as he sat in a lawn chair reading the sports page and listening to the ballgame he never said, although surely he must have noted there was some pace to my hitting stones that matched the play-by-play on the radio. Also, it was our custom in those days to play a game of catch after the "radio game" — as he called it — was over. Throwing the ball back and forth, my father would from time to time toss me a "grounder" to one side or the other, and if I fielded it well he'd say: *That's a Phil Rizzuto for you. That's a Pee Wee Reese.*

On fly balls I'd be Joe DiMaggio or — because my father was a Red Sox fan, due to his deep admiration for Ted Williams's service in the Korean War — I could become, when I caught up with one of his tossed deep drives, a Dom DiMaggio. *That's a Dom DiMaggio. Do you know who Dom DiMaggio is?* As Dom DiMaggio was not on the radio in Kansas City, I did not. *He's the forgotten brother of Joe, just like Korea will be the forgotten war,* my father would say. *Don't forget the forgotten.*

If I muffed the grounder or dropped the long fly, my father would throw one in just the same way — and he would do this until I fielded it correctly. In this way all my errors on our front lawn cum Kansas City Blues fantasy baseball field were swept clean, so that my play seemed as spotless as a new uniform or a freshly dusted home plate.

But while my father indulged me (and perhaps himself) in our imitation baseball games, it is true as well that he was the one who, a few summers later (it was the same summer we discussed — in a roundabout way — the origin of puppies), broke the bubble of illusion about radio games and told me that the out-of-town baseball I was listening to on these Saturday and Sunday afternoons was broadcast not from, say, Minneapolis, where the games were in fact being played, but from a building in Kansas City, complete with prerecorded crowd noise and bat whacks. The announcers, my father asserted, were describing the Bob Cervs and the Cliff Mapeses and Ralph Houks from a ticker tape they were getting in the studio near the radio tower that I could see at night out of my bedroom window blinking, blinking in the distance, twenty or so miles to the east.

I remember my hitting stick was in my hand when my father told me the true nature of the radio baseball broadcasts. Mickey Mantle (who had been sent to the minors briefly by the Yankees) had just doubled to right. A double to right was tricky business on my field. You had to put it between a cottonwood tree in right center and a dead ash tree that marked the right field foul line and in which a mother blue jay was raising her young. Beyond that, you had to hit a pile of rubble that was an abandoned car and various other metal junk, which would ping to signal your two-base hit. Before I pitched up my stone for my left-handed swing (like Mantle, I could hit from both sides of the plate), I hesitated. What was I hitting? Was it a stone or a ball? *Next up is the catcher...* Where was I hitting it? Into the right field fence or into a pile of Studebaker rubble? Who was on first? Was that Ralph Houk coming up or Bobby Day? What was the score? Who was I? *What's the matter, son?* Not a thing, I think now, as long as I can imagine the game for myself. Television, I have learned, is the real enemy of reality.

Home Run Baker, 1995

"I once met Frank Baker," Ed Athey says to me. We are sitting in the third base dugout at Kibler Field on the Washington College campus. The college team has not yet come out for practice. The day is warm. The dogwoods are in full bloom; the campus lilac bushes are beginning to blush. The infield grass is clipped and the base paths have been freshly dragged. The pitcher's mound looks lonely without me. I have come to ask for my old job back but worry I won't have the nerve.

Tom Kibler (for whom the field is named) was Ed Athey's coach, and once president of the Eastern Shore League. Kibler and Baker had played ball together. The history of baseball is, like most histories, linked to the past by a series of serendipitous handshakes. I am about to learn that the man whose hand I shook by way of greeting earlier this afternoon has shaken the hand of Home Run Baker, who in his turn no doubt shook hands with Walter Johnson, into whose glove William Howard Taft (the first president to throw out an opening day ball) once tossed a slow fat one at the Washington Senators' National Park (at Seventh and Florida Avenues) to start the 1910 season.

"What was he like?" I say. "Home Run Baker. What was he like?"

"Big," says Ed. "I remember thinking when he came out of his home in Trappe, 'That's a big, rawboned man.' He had a ruddy outdoor quality to him. He might have been a farmer who worked in the fields all day, he looked so strong and healthy. I can see his face now. Stern. Like he was still trying to get a hit."

"Did you talk baseball?"

"He talked baseball with Coach Kibler," says Ed. "We were giving

Baker a ride to Salisbury for an award by the Eastern Shore League. I sat in the back seat all the way down and all the way back but I sat forward in it and right in the middle so I could hear everything they said. They talked about home runs and about how soft the ball was when Frank Baker played. He seemed to remember one home run in particular. I think it was toward the end of his career."

"Did you ever see Ruth play?" I ask. "I did," says Ed Athey. "I saw him on a barnstorming tour over in Cumberland, Maryland. He was playing in the Wineow Street stadium. He was with a whole team of major leaguers whose names you could find in any baseball book today, but I can't remember anybody but Ruth. You knew him the minute you saw him. He filled the field."

"Did he homer?"

"He did. And it was the longest home run he ever hit."

"How do they know?" I ask.

"Because it went over the right field fence and landed in a coal car that was passing through on the tracks that ran just outside the stadium. The ball probably went another hundred miles before it touched ground." Here Ed laughs in delight at the story.

"Did you see it land in the coal car?" I ask.

"I did not," says Ed. "I was sitting too low in the stands to see the trains go by the outfield fence. I could hear them, though. But you had to sit up higher to see Ruth's homer land in the train. Somebody told me that's what happened. I don't even know if it's true."

"I would have seen it," I say. "No matter where I had been sitting. I can see it now. It bounces once when it hits the coal and raises a puff of dust."

"That's why you're a writer," says Ed.

The Author, 1950

The summer I was eight, my father took me down to the Cub Scout ballpark for the tryouts. That would be the year I started playing baseball for real instead of just in the radio games I banged out at the end of my driveway (although those would continue for many years).

"What position do you want to play?" my father asked as we were driving to the field.

"Batter," I said.

"Everybody's a hitter," he said. "You have to play some other position."

"I just want to bat," I said. "I don't want to play another postion."

This was all before television and before I had ever seen a real game of baseball. Hearing games over the radio and playing catch with my father, I of course understood in some dim way that there were players other than batters.

"You play in the field for half an inning and then you bat for the other," he said.

"I don't want to," I said. What parents never seem to understand about children is how much their world is shaped by themselves. And how little of it they are willing to explain by way of explanation: How to tell my father that only hitters mattered because in the game at the end of the driveway (which was the only game going in my mind), I was always the batter. And I was all batters just as he was all fathers. How to be other than ourselves?

"We'll see," said my father.

What we saw (what I saw) was that the game, as played on a field other than my own, had as its author a player who stood on a mound of brown dirt with a white dash running partway across it — and that I wanted to be that author. Did I think that then? I must have: I think it now. How else to explain that puff of coal dust rising from Ruth's home run?

The Ball: Circa 1990

A number of years ago, Amos, my Labrador Retriever, made the national news for his ability to sniff out and retrieve all kinds of lost balls in the raspberry and blackberry patches that border the athletic fields at Washington College. Mainly he retrieved lacrosse balls, nearly a thousand over a ten-year stretch. But he also found softballs (ten), soccer balls (two — he pushed them out of the weeds with his nose) and baseballs (a hundred or so). One of those baseballs was an especially old and black one with its cover badly torn so that you could see the string inside. I saved it to give to Ed Athey at a celebration in his honor when he retired as athletic director.

"I have in my hand," I said when it came my turn to speak, "the last ball Ed ever hit out of the park at Kibler Field as a player for Washington College. That was on June 4th, 1942, at 2:32 in the afternoon. Amos retrieved it just this week. It was buried so deep in the weeds it took him an hour to dig it out." There was some general laughter and a round of applause.

"That dog saved us a bit of money over the years," said Ed, looking at the beaten-up old ball I had just given him. "And we sure are grateful," he went on, now beginning to turn the ball around in his hand as if studying a lineup card. "But I have to say, I don't think this is the last ball I hit out. I think I went and got that one back myself."

In my mind's eye, I am throwing the pitch Ed hit: It is my Ewell Blackwell side-arm cross-fire, this time with a screwball tacked onto the end so that after it drives Ed out of the box, it sneaks back over the plate for a strike. But the pitch is so slow that Ed can recover before it slips into the catcher's mitt. He hits it halfway to the graveyard. Somewhere I hear the whistle of a coal train coming down the tracks.

Sorrento, Italy, Circa 1953

I am standing at the end of a jetty that goes out into the Mediterranean. I have found myself an Italian hitting stick, a smooth piece of driftwood. With it I am hitting line drives and towering home runs into the water. Center field is Sardinia, right field is Corsica and left field is Capri (we have been studying world geography in grade school, and one of the conditions my parents have placed on me during this

— our first trip to Europe — is that I know both where I am and where I have been).

Where I have been during the previous hour is hitting stones into the sea while my mother and father amble the streets and poke among the shops of Sorrento itself. (My father, by the way, in Rome the previous day, has sung "Come Back to Sorrento" to my mother at Alfredo's restaurant in his fine Irish tenor voice and to the complete amazement and no doubt embarrassment of Alfredo's American tourist patrons, but to the great delight of the Italian waiters — and of Alfredo himself who has given my mother the pasta bowl out of which he has dispensed his fettuccine).

It is nearly sundown as I make my way toward the end of the game. Yogi Berra (the Kansas City Blues have given way to the 1953 New York Yankees, and without a radio I am playing my own games in my own mind) has just singled toward the coast of France. Cannes, no doubt. Hank Bauer (who doubled toward Tunis) has come home.

About half an hour before, I have noticed some small boys playing soccer on the beach. Now they are coming up the jetty, keeping their ball in front of them with their feet. My hitting is about to draw a crowd, albeit a tiny one, and of course one that will have to cheer me on in Italian.

Giving up Gene Woodling (he hits sixth in my lineup) for some general outfield fungos, I rap a few flies into the water. A boy kicks the soccer ball gently in my direction. I put my foot out to stop it, but it rolls past me. Everybody laughs.

The boy who kicked me the ball makes a waving motion with his arm, something like hitting. I give him my bat, pick up a few stones from the jetty and give them to him as well. He looks at me for a moment, then tosses one tentatively in the air, swings, and misses. He tries again: no luck. I don't feel so bad about the soccer ball. Five strikes later, he pops up. In my mind's eye Billy Martin catches it with ease around second base.

"DiMaggio," he says to me as he gives me back the bat. I give him his soccer ball which I have picked up. "DiMaggio," he says again, pointing at me.

"DiMaggio," says one of the boys from the group there on the jetty. They all point at me. "DiMaggio."

I pick up some stones, sorting through them to find good round ones. Facing the sea, I open my stance in imitation of the Yankee Clipper, even though he is not on my team.

"DiMaggio," I say.

"DiMaggio," they say.

I toss up my best stone and hit a towering drive well over Andy Pafko in left field and into the bleachers of Alexandria. Grace under pressure. Everybody cheers.

The Stretch, Now and Then — and in the Future

Probably more than half of the text of baseball writing is statistics. Readers of The Sports Encyclopedia of Baseball (Expanded, Revised and Updated), Grosset and Dunlap, 1981 (it's the most recent edition I have), will find a hundred pages of statistics for every page of prose. (Sloppy Thurston on page 141, for example, a right handed pitcher for the Chicago White Sox in 1924, was at that time twenty-five years old. Among his other thirteen statistical accomplishments, he pitched one shutout and had an earned run average of 3.80.) In baseball, immortality in print is a matter of lines in the tables, not volumes on the shelf — much less home runs that land in coal cars or on the beaches of Corsica. Put another way, baseball statistics are the ultimate factual prose, the epitome of nonfiction. Truth itself. Ah, truth.

My own statistical life is more dubious, mainly because I am the author of it both on the field and off: in the book and out. Full disclosure here: Everything I have written thus far is true the way radio baseball is true, including the following table:

Player: Day, Robert

Position: Batter (1950-1950); Pitcher (1950 to present); Writer (1950 to present)

Teams: Kansas City Radios (1949 to present); New York Yankees (1953 to present); Sorrento All Stars (1953 to present); Washington College Sho'men (1972 to present).
Won/Lost: Yes.

The Ball, 1953-1995

There is a baseball on the desk where I write. It has the autographs of the 1953 Yankees: Allie Reynolds, Ewell Blackwell, Mickey Mantle, Phil Rizzuto, Casey Stengel, Larry Berra, Hank Bauer, Vic Raschi, Gil McDougald, Frank Crosetti, among others. Like some writers I know who touch wood to keep their game going, I touch the ball to coach my paragraphs around the bases. It is my hope that the signatures will not fade before I do.

My father and I bought the ball from a vendor (it was the last in his case) in Yankee Stadium one Sunday afternoon: two dollars from my father's wallet and all three dollars from a roll of one-dollar bills bound tightly by a rubber band and kept in my right front jeans pocket. It was what was left of the five dollars I had brought as my allowance all the way from Kansas City to New York.

We had seen the balls for sale on the way in — or at least I had. All through the game (which Vic Raschi pitched and the Yankees won) I remembered those balls: They filled up the field in my mind even as the players who had signed them filled the field in front of me.

Between innings four and five my father and I left our seats to get some peanuts, and I went one stall down to look again at the balls, now much fewer in number. During the seventh-inning stretch, I went on my own to the men's room and stopped by the ball vendor to look once again. He was down to two balls. He pulled one out of the case and put it on the counter. I could see that Phil Rizzuto had signed just beneath Ray Scarborough. I touched my three dollars in my pocket and wished I had five.

After the game, my father led me to the vendor who had the baseballs. There was one left.

"You want to sell the boy that ball," my father said.

"He's been looking at it," said the man as he took the ball out of the case and spun it around on the top of the counter, then tossed it to me. "Do you throw your fastball with the seams or across them?" he asked.

"Across them," I said, putting my index finger and middle finger across Tom Gorman and Casey Stengel.

"You'll get better movement with the seams," said the man.

"How much?" said my father. Maybe he was hoping for a sale price at the end of the game.

"Five dollars," said the man. "Five dollars and you'll never forget it. Cheap for a memory."

He was right about that.

The Windup, 1995

You don't need a batting practice pitcher this year, do you?" I say in such a way that Ed Athey won't think I'm serious. His players are coming out from the locker room for practice. Some of them are beginning to toss the ball around. The mound looks lonely without me.

Ed gets up and we step outside the dugout. He points over the roof toward where the train tracks cut through the back half of the campus. The coal train has passed taking Babe Ruth's homer with it. Behind us I can hear the swish, swish of two strikes, then the thump of a drive hit into the Chester River. I see myself catching the opening day pitch from President Taft, the 1953 Yankees gathered on the field behind me. In the first inning Berra will hit a double into an abandoned Studebaker in right. Mantle will follow with a long drive in the direction of Tunis.

"You see that graveyard," Ed says.

"There are arms over there," I say, "that..."

Writers always get to throw the final pitch.

A LONG GOODBYE

THE LAST SKIPJACKS

Tom Horton

LATE IN THE LAST CENTURY the *Rebecca T. Ruark* was launched on Maryland's Eastern Shore to dredge the oysters of Chesapeake Bay, a pursuit that by 1886 had assumed all the frenzy of the California gold rush. As *Rebecca*'s massive oaken keel was laid, thousands of sailcraft were stripping 15 million bushels of oysters from the bay bottom — a yield of edible meat, it was calculated, equal to 160,000 prime steers.

Few thought then the greatest shellfish bounty on the planet ever could be depleted. In fact, Chesapeake oyster harvests would never again attain the peaks of the wide-open 1880s; but as recently as 1975 the great estuary that stretches 200 miles from Norfolk to the Pennsylvania line still yielded a third of the nation's oysters, with catches still in the low millions of bushels.

But now, in more recent seasons, the unthinkable is happening. It's autumn, a season that richly overlaps all that's central to pleasant living on the Chesapeake — fresh blue crabs steamed for dinner and raw, salty oysters as the appetizer; striped bass are still biting, and goose season's open too; loons and swans yodel on the coves, coon dogs bay in the night woods. Grain combines lumber across waterfront farms, shelling corn into glistening, brassy mounds; and the white canvas of the oyster dredgers, North America's last fleet of working sailcraft, puts a fine, bright exclamation point on the whole affair.

At 3:30 A.M., under the glare of lights in a marina across the bay from Baltimore, *Rebecca* and half a dozen other old skipjacks, as the dredgeboats are called, rock and creak to a rising wind. Amid acres of lustrous chrome and fiberglass pleasurecraft they seem like a relict species, rangy Longhorns of Texas trail drives corralled with modern, fatted Herefords and Angus. *Minnie V., Thomas Clyde, H.M. Krentz, Virginia W.* — fully a third of the twenty or so skipjacks that remain from the glory days of a century past are in this one spot.

Although this is the heart of the oyster season, only *Rebecca*, the oldest of the fleet, and maybe one other boat plan to sail today, and that more from stubborn habit than expectation of catching anything worthwhile. And this is why you have crawled from bed at 2:00 A.M. and driven here on what promises to be a nasty day, cold rain and slashing wind. Because the harvests that once were 15 million bushels have begun to slide over the edge, it seems, of no return. Last season, from October 1991 to April 1992, the catch for the entire Maryland bay was about 350,000 bushels, a historic low. This season is going to make that harvest look flush.

What more than a century of overfishing, mismanagement and pollution began, virulent oyster diseases during the last decade threaten to finish. Today, or one day pretty soon, though there are months left to oyster, the last skipjack is going to quit sail dredging for the season; and maybe forever. So today, although it is not convenient, and though you have gone many times before, you are going; because who would miss a last chance to ride on a beautiful dinosaur?

Geese are piping up a faint glow in the east when gravel crunches under the tires of Captain Wade Murphy's pickup. Wadey is a Tilghman Islander, from a fishing community midway down the bayside of the Eastern Shore. The island is turning trendier every year with the vacation homes of Washington, Baltimore and Annapolis. His family has been dredging the bay almost as long as *Rebecca*. Wadey, at fifty-one, is in his thirty-fifth year as a captain. He got her at the age of 100 from an old captain named Emerson Todd, who wept when she sailed away.

Emerson, Wadey says this morning, has died and is being buried today. It was one funeral he would very much have liked to attend, but the wind was supposed to hold at fifteen knots from the southwest at least through early afternoon, and if you were not going to go dredging oysters on such days, then whenever were you? Emerson would understand.

"I never dreamed I would see it get like this." Wadey is almost apologetic about our chances of finding oysters today. Only a few years ago, this early in the season, the crew might have been speculating how close they would come to the legal, 150 bushel a day limit for dredgers. Today, his regular crew slept in. Almost since the season began they have refused to work any but the two "push days" — Monday and Tuesday.

In recent decades the state has relaxed its sail-only law for oyster dredging, letting the skipjacks employ the small but high-powered "push" boats they carry hung from their sterns. Power dredging is to sail dredging what house painting is to portraiture — little art to the former — but you cover lots of territory, and it has been the salvation of the old craft as oysters declined. The spirit, if not the letter, of the push-days allowance requires the skipjacks the rest of the week to sail, a sight that to most Marylanders is as evocative of the winter Chesapeake as flights of waterfowl. But increasingly now, many of the boats are making a mockery of the loophole, working only on power days. One has never even bothered to finish putting on its sails this season.

Wadey is made of sterner stuff. He comes from what you might call the Edward Harrison school of thought. Ed is a legendary bay softcrabber who has personally provided the market with millions of softcrab sandwiches in his seventy-year career. Younger softcrabbers have told Ed you must learn to treat their profession as a business, not a way of life — when the weather is bad and crabs are scarce, careful calculation may show you can save money by staying in port. Ed says he figures a man out there in his crab boat *always* has a better chance of getting the crab than a man home in bed.

Today, Wadey has assembled a makeshift crew: his boy, Wade 3d, a strapping youth of twenty who would like to be the fourth generation of Murphys to captain a skipjack, but knows he never will, and Allen Harrison, a young Tilghman Islander who says Wade 3d recruited him out of a bar at 4:30 A.M., but who seems able and ready to dredge. "We are basically playing with our peckers, being out here," he says good naturedly; "finding oysters now is like hunting pterodactyls... this is the last of it."

Another of the four-man crew says he had been trying to catch oysters with his father using hand tongs, wire baskets attached to long, wooden shafts operated scissorlike to scrape oysters a few at a time from the bay bottom. The gear is only slightly evolved from what Native Americans used. Although the skipjacks are the most visible symbols of bay oystering, it is tonging with both manual and hydraulic powered equipment from smaller craft, that employs the great bulk of the bay's oystermen. The crewman says his best catch amounted to three bushels, about sixty dollars for a hard day's work, before deducting for gas and splitting it with his dad.

As *Rebecca* reaches the open bay this morning, Wadey says he will be picking over bottom that has been dredged and tonged a thousand times already this year. Just a little "lump," a tiny patch of undiscovered oysters, is all he hopes for, enough to make a day's pay for his crew.

From behind *Rebecca*'s wheel, the captain can peer down into the small cabin, heated by the open burners of an old gas stove. Strewn with oilskins and boots and drying gloves, the interior would seem familiar to the boat's first crew in 1886; all except for the video screen on which every nuance of the bay's bottom is rendered in vivid reds and blues and greens. In his home waters around the Choptank river, Wadey says, he would not need electronic aids; but for the first time in living memory, the oysters there are all dead. In the less familiar territory of the upper bay, the video helps considerably.

And now it shows *Rebecca* passing over a small rise in the bottom, possibly oysters, but so small that in normal times it would not be worth trying. "Ho wind'ard!" the captain shouts, and the crew heaves over the heavy iron dredge on the upwind side of the boat.

By feeling the vibrations coming up through the steel dredge cable, a practiced crewman can tell whether the boat is on barren mud or oysters, and even tell live oysters from oyster shell. And now Allen Harrison, excited, yells: "Cap'n she's hittin!" A small motor forward on the deck winds in the dredge, large enough to hold a man in its chain mesh bag. Sixty oysters — it is, Wadey says, "the best lick we've made in a long time."

You can see the crew's minds doing the math as they hop to cull live from dead shellfish and get the dredges back to work. Roughly, the number of oysters you average per dredge translates into the number of bushels you can catch in a day. Sixty times $24, the going market, equals $1,440, minus the one third the captain takes for "the boat," minus expenses, the rest divided by captain and crew — a solid $200 apiece; and for awhile it does look that good.

By modern standards a skipjack is a clumsy beast at forty tons, with a beam nearly a third its forty-five to fifty-foot length, its huge mainsail designed more for torque to plow the bay bottom than for nimbleness and easy handling; but all that vanishes now, as *Rebecca* does what she was born for. Against all odds, Wadey has gotten into the oystering equivalent of what sports people call the "sweet spot," that certain grooved swing of a racket or a bat or a club where contact makes the ball rocket away, imbued with an almost otherworldly energy. The feeling, if you have ever hit it, is unforgettable.

No need now for the video recorder. With a few passes across the lump, Wadey has gotten its invisible contours down in his head better than you could imagine your backyard. The wind is filling the sails, driving the dredges at just the right speed to gorge on oysters. The tide is giving *Rebecca* just the right counterbalance to hold her up to the wind, and she is licking across that oyster bed and coming about smartly and licking back again; and the captain is hollering, "whooooah!" to wind and heave the dredges every few seconds, it seems; and the crew is culling and shoveling like crazy men — a perfect synchrony of wind, tide, boat, crew, captain and bay bottom — skimming oysters off that hidden bottom as neatly as you'd shave your whiskers.

Wadey, always the perfectionist, says if he had his regular crew he'd be catching oysters twice as fast; but his face radiates a deep satisfaction. This is more than he expected. As the oysters pile on deck he talks about how he mortgaged his modest home a few years ago to pour nearly $70,000 into taking the rotten wood out of *Rebecca*, preparing her to oyster for a second century. He was advised by most to save money and "C-Flex her," simply wrap her worn timbers in a patented encapsulation system of fiberglass.

"But I respect what the old captains say, and they said fiberglass is dead, wood works, it's live; you wrap her up in glass and you've killed the life out of her."

He's been reading a book, he says, about the old oyster schooners of Delaware Bay, which lost its oysters long before the Chesapeake. "It talks about how bad those old timers felt when they finally cut the spars (masts) outa 'em and went to straight power. Some of 'em here on the Chesapeake wouldn't care if we did that tomorrow, but that's no way to oyster," he says, biting the words off hard.

The sweet spot fades as suddenly as it came on. A line in *Rebecca*'s rigging snaps, requiring an hour to fix, and by then the wind and tide have made it impossible to sail the proper line of attack to dredge the lump. The crew has downgraded the day's pay but will still make more than a hundred dollars apiece.

* * *

Now it is March, the last full month of oyster season, and across tens of thousands of acres of oyster beds, scarcely a tonger or a dredger is working. A waterfowl researcher, out censusing loons, tells of being waved over by several tongers as he cruised his skiff up a creek bounded by large estates. "Sir, do you have any work?" they ask, taking him for one of the landed gentry.

Preliminary harvest projections indicate the take may not reach

120,000 bushels. That is only a third of the previous historic low. It is less than one percent of historic peak harvests of a century ago. Oyster shucking houses around the bay — the few that remain open — are buying more and more of their oysters from Gulf and West Coast states. Repackaged, they are then legally sold as "fresh Maryland oysters."

Debate and controversy abound over what should be done to replenish the treasure house that Native Americans knew as "the great shellfish bay." Such concern is scarcely new: "I am of the opinion that the fecundity of the beds… is very much impaired, and that their total failure is but a question of time," said Naval Lieutenant Francis Winslow after making a definitive survey of the Chesapeake's oysters — in 1879. In 1993 Winslow's warning seems near coming true, despite decades of reports, blue ribbon commissions, scientific inquiries and conservation laws aimed at conserving oysters. It is particularly ironic that the demise of such a hallmark species has occurred in the last decade, which has seen an unprecedented multi-state and federal effort to restore the Chesapeake's water quality and natural resources after severe declines that began in the 1960s.

The restoration program, frequently cited as a model for the future, has attracted national and international attention since it was launched in 1983, the same year blue crabs replaced oysters for the first time in history as the Chesapeake's most valuable commercial catch.

The program's scope extends throughout most of a drainage basin, or watershed, that sprawls from Cooperstown, New York, nearly to North Carolina, and from Pendleton county, West Virginia, nearly to the Atlantic. Its ambitious commitments include a permanent cap on sewage discharges, no matter how much population increases, and reducing polluted runoff from farms as far upstream from the bay as central Pennsylvania and Virginia's Shenandoah Valley; also breaching dozens of dams to restore historic spawning runs of bay species to as far as Binghamton, New York.

None of this seems to have helped the oyster, however. In fact, one lesson learned in a decade of trying to restore the bay is that fisheries disputes can be among the most intractable of environmental problems. That is particularly true with Crassostrea virginica, the species of oyster native to the Chesapeake and other coastal states from Maine to Texas. On the land, as long ago as the development of agriculture, society began moving toward the concepts of individual ownership and private rights.

But not on the rich submerged lands that form the Chesapeake oyster beds. They have for the most part remained zealously guarded as a commons, open to all citizens, perpetuating lifestyles among bay "watermen" that remain closer to hunter-gatherers than anything of our modern age. The images of men and boats still attuned more to natural forces than to time clocks is no small part of the reason the skipjack is Maryland's official state boat, and why scenes of tonging and dredging for oysters adorn the region, from art museums to place mats in diners.

An old skipjack crewman, asked once about "the romance" of oystering, said: "Romantic? Yeah, that it were — wakin' up on your bunk under them leaky decks with your hair stuck by frost to the planks. After thirty years aboard somebody give me a sleeping bag, and I thought that was fine livin'." But the reality notwithstanding, for most of the public, the romance looms large.

The prescient Lt. Winslow more than a century ago wrote that he found "one cause" ran like a thread through the destruction of oyster fisheries from Europe to New England: "The fishery has been common property, its preservation everybody's business — that is, nobody's — and consequently it has not been preserved."

And so it is that even as it declined, the common oyster resource has been increasingly divided among more interests, ranging from scuba divers to "patent tongers," who use hydraulic power to crunch the oyster beds with massive tongs weighing hundreds of pounds, a practice widely thought to be destructive. Push days for the skipjacks, modern fishfinder and navigation technology — even recent court rulings that allowed oystermen to range outside their own county's shellfish areas — have added pressure on the common resource.

Until the last decade or two, these and most decisions regarding oyster conservation were made more with the political clout of watermen in mind than with regard to biological implications. In a 1981 review, "Sixteen Decades of Political Management of the Oyster Fishery," Victor S. Kennedy, a University of Maryland marine researcher, concluded, "A century's accumulation of scientific insights, commission recommendations and general popular support of private oyster culture has been negated to a great extent by political sensitivity to an influential, vocal minority." Many watermen themselves will concede that working in a commons, where someone else (or a natural predator, or a disease) may well get whatever you forgo, drives them to "take the last oyster." In 1991 a number of patent tongers proved in court that the state had incorrectly marked a small oyster sanctuary meant to preserve some spawning stock, and proceeded to wipe it out in a few days. Yet the symbolism of the waterman's way of life remains powerful enough that perserving it is promoted by both government and environmental groups as a major reason for restoring the bay's health.

Further complicating the debate over the Chesapeake oyster's future is the spectre of two parasites that have periodically erupted throughout most of the bay during the last thirty years. Neither is harmful to humans, but they invade the oyster and feed on its tissues, causing it to literally waste away. Recently they have become epidemic, killing oysters everywhere but the uppermost portions of the bay and its tidal rivers, where fresher water seems to stop their spread.

Virtually everyone agrees that the main force driving the precipitous decline of oysters in the last decade has been the two diseases, known as MSX and Dermo. But state fisheries managers in Maryland and Virginia go a controversial step further, saying in effect that disease is the only problem, and rejecting calls from environmentalists and scientists to shut down or restrict watermens' harvests.

The best management policy, state officials say, with no cure or disease-resistant oyster on the horizon, is to keep oystering and try to "manage around" the parasites by moving surviving young oysters from saltier parts of the bay to fresher parts, where they have a better chance to grow to the legal catch limit of three inches.

William P. Jensen, the top fisheries manager for Maryland's Department of Natural Resources, flatly denies there is a problem with overfishing. He claims there are nearly as many oysters in the Chesapeake now as there were a century ago. Old harvest records, he thinks, are greatly overstated; and limited research by his department shows present populations of young oysters are probably as dense as they ever were — the problem is just that disease is killing them before they get big enough for legal harvest (because they do get large enough to reproduce before dying, the diseases don't threaten the oyster with extermination).

Such a view simplifies the oyster situation so far as to strain credibility, in the opinion of several shellfish biologists who have issued studies of their own in the last year. Today's bay has less than half the habitat for oysters than it did a century ago, simply from physical destruction of the beds, according to researchers at the University of Maryland's Center for Environmental and Estuarine Studies. This began in the 1870s with the breakup by dredging of the large reefs, or "rocks" in which oysters naturally grew. Anecdotal accounts from Colonial times tell of ships grounding on such reefs at low tide. Up to a point, scattering the reefs was possibly beneficial, as the oysters, spread out on the bottom, grew larger and faster; but ultimately this flattening of the rocks, compounded in modern times by heavy patent tongs, may have made oysters more susceptible to smothering by sediment and other pollution stresses, which in turn might have made them more susceptible to disease.

Thus, even the oyster habitat that remains is often of low quality, the report says. Scientists also worry that continued harvesting is removing from the gene pool the very oysters that are able to grow fastest to legal size, or otherwise avoid succumbing to the deadly diseases. They also question the current practice of moving oysters from salty, disease-prone waters to fresher parts of the bay, saying it probably is spreading disease. "It is one thing, if you could go back to [the 1960s] when they began moving oysters, you'd probably change," says Dr. Kennedy.

A more profound issue has been raised by Roger Newell, a University of Maryland oyster expert who has forced a rethinking of the very role of the oyster. Regarded since the Civil War primarily as a commercial resource and a tasty hors d'oeuvre, the oyster may in fact have played a critical part in regulating bay water quality.

The shellfish are superb filters, feeding on plankton in the water by gaping their shells slightly and sucking up to two gallons of water per hour through their gills. This removes significant quantities of sediment and plankton, clarifying the water; and the nutrient-rich feces the feeding oyster deposits on the bottom form the basis of an important food web that ultimately supports fish and crabs.

Dr. Newell has calculated that the pre-1870 stocks of bay oysters had the capacity to filter every few days a volume of water equal to the whole, 18-trillion gallon Chesapeake. The filtering capacity of today's diminished shellfish beds, he says, would take most of a year to do the same job.

What that means is that the loss of bay oysters may have meant the loss of far more than income from fishing. The equivalent of a major biological filtration system has been impaired. It is quite possible, Dr. Newell concluded in a recent paper, that this loss of living filters has contributed to the huge excesses of plankton that cloud the modern bay's waters and, when they die and decompose, cause severe oxygen losses in the deep channels.

Maryland's Mr. Jensen has dismissed Newell's estimates that oysters now provide as little as one percent of their historical filtering capacity as "fantasy," but many experts find his assumptions quite plausible. "We can debate whether we're down to one percent... whether the main problem is disease or overfishing, but we've got to accept the ecological value of the oyster," says Steve Nelson.

There is increasing interest nationally among ecologists about "top down" pollution control — that is, restoring natural pollution filters like marshes and forests, seagrass beds and shellfish to absorb the contaminants we now focus only on controlling from the "bottom up," with methods like sewage treatment, manure holding tanks on farms, and regulation of industrial discharges.

The idea of oysters as ecosystem filters has caught the interest of both water quality managers and environmentalists, who see it as a new and compelling reason to restore shellfish in the bay. And among waterfront homeowners near Annapolis, Maryland, it has even become fashionable to maintain a few bushels of oysters off one's dock to help, if only symbolically, restore water quality.

Dr. Newell echoes many experts, however, when he says there are no easy or quick fixes for the oyster problem, and maybe no fixes at all. Scientists still have only a poor grasp of how the parasites causing dermo disease and MSX kill oysters; and no one yet even knows how MSX spreads or where it retreats in years when high rainfall reduces the bay's salinity enough to give the oysters temporary respite. The initial outbreak of MSX in the 1960s, when a drought made the bay ususually salty, triggered a flow of research money, Dr. Kennedy says, "but the 1970s were wet... the problem seemed to go away, and research money dried up." Dry years in the '80s brought disease roaring back, and eventually, more than a million dollars a year in research funding. The diseases do not have any effect on humans who eat infected oysters.

Recently, state oyster officials have been prodded sharply by Bill Matuszeski, director of the EPA Chesapeake Bay Program that oversees and coordinates restoration of the estuary: "The pervasive feeling seems to be that the states are essentially administering last rites to a dying patient. The can-do has gone out of the management system; the goal seems to be to get through another year without a major further decline...." There are signs that both Maryland and Virginia, shaken by the latest low harvests, may be willing to reassess their current management programs. In Virginia's Piankatank River, James Wesson, a waterman, Ph.D. ecologist and now head of oyster repletion for the state, is going to construct from scratch an oyster reef such as the ships of the colonists talked of grounding on.

He will use 170,000 bushels of shell to make a structure 1,000 feet long and 100 feet wide, high enough to break the river's surface at low tide, and let it colonize naturally as larval oysters attach to its nooks and crannies. He sees this and other efforts more as "experiments... not something that's going to turn oysters around; but we're at Custer's Last Stand here, and we might as well try something." Virginia's latest harvests stand at less than 60,000 bushels, down from 110,000 just two years ago.

Maryland's Department of Natural Resources is organizing an "oyster *charrette*," a summit meeting of scientists, watermen, managers and environmentalists that will, according to one official, "put everything on the board," including the possibility of closing all or part of the bay to harvest. Dr. Newell notes that in more than a century, "no one has ever been willing to choose a number and say, 'this is the end point' — below this level of harvest we cannot accept continued fishing. Until that happens, a meaningful debate over the oyster's future really cannot begin. We will just continue to drift."

One solution gaining momentum in recent years has been to forget the bay oyster and introduce an Asian species, Crassostrea gigas, which is now the basis for a thriving private oyster-growing industry in the Pacific Northwest. Gigas is not affected by the bay's oyster diseases. Virginia, with its oysters so depleted it has virtually nothing to lose, was on the verge of experimenting with the exotic oyster last year. But Maryland, both out of concerns that gigas could overwhelm the native oysters, and watermens' fears of private industry invading their historic commons, pressured its southern neighbor to back off, pending more research.

Watermen remain a potent force resisting radical changes in management of the shellfish; but that clout may be fading rapidly. Harvest statistics from Maryland indicate that more than two-thirds of the state's 2,500 licensed oystermen are now grossing less than a thousand dollars a year for their efforts (catching less than fifty bushels annually, a number that not long ago was achievable in a day or two).

Fewer than ten percent of the oystermen are grossing more than $10,000 for a winter's work; and those incomes are based on harvests nearly three times those of the season just concluded, for which statistics are not available yet. Many oystermen say they do not think next year will even be worth the expense of gearing up to go tonging and dredging. "I think you may have almost a de-facto moratorium in many places," one oyster scientist says.

The end of traditional oyster harvesting from the greatest oyster trove that ever existed seems close, and with it a fundamental change in the Chesapeake scene. The skipjacks, unlike the smaller, all-purpose workboats of watermen who tong and dive for oysters, were built for one thing only — dredging oysters — and if that goes, it would seem the old dredge boats must go too.

But maybe not entirely. As the season ends, Wadey Murphy says he plans to begin hitting the books, a scarier task for most watermen than sailing through a hurricane. He is going to take the arduous Coast Guard exam to become a licensed captain, allowed to carry paying passengers. *Rebecca* must also pass federal safety inspections, a tough task for a century-old wooden craft. A few other skipjack captains are also thinking about outfitting for the tourist trade; maybe even for environmental education trips. A foundation in Baltimore now is offering beleaguered skipjack captains free repairs in hopes of keeping the boats afloat, if only for festivals and parades.

Wadey says recently he took a group of scuba diving enthusiasts out "sport oystering" — two-bushel limit per person. Another time a man and his wife asked could they just sail on *Rebecca* and help the crew with the grinding task of culling oysters as they came aboard in the dredges. "They wanted to pay me $100 to let 'em work," Wadey says incredulously.

Between the tourists and crabbing all summer in his smaller powerboat he hopes he can keep *Rebecca* going, the captain says. Crabs are still healthy in the Chesapeake, though watermen and scientists alike worry about how the pressure on them is skyrocketing as oysters and other species founder. In the last decade or so the number of crab pots, or traps, set in the bay has gone from about 600,000 to a million, and still rising.

You hope they make it, Wadey and *Rebecca* and the other dredgers; but even if they do, it will never be the same. You recall that last sail day aboard Rebecca, as Wadey came to dock with a hard-won thirty-nine bushels, thirty-six more than the only other skipjack that even tried. "I am going to miss this," he murmured. "So… damn… bad."

BAY BLUES

David Finkel

IN THE CONTINUING SAGA of what we have come to know as the gasping, suffocating, fish-deficient, oyster-hostile, algae-infested, sediment-choked, sewage-bloated, terminally ill Chesapeake Bay, there was, on a recent evening, a perfect moment, a suggestion of how enticing the bay continues to be.

It happened at Port Isobel, a tiny island in the wide waters just south of the Maryland-Virginia line. It was nearly dark, nearly warm, nearly summer. The sky was turning purple. The first stars were out. On a dock, Keith Bjerke stood taking it all in, while in the background Frances Flanigan couldn't help but wonder what he was thinking.

For several years, Flanigan had been trying to get someone like Bjerke out on the bay. He is a high-level administrator in the U.S. Department of Agriculture, she is executive director of the Alliance for the Chesapeake Bay. He knows only a little about the bay, and she knows almost everything, including the fact that a significant cause of the bay's deterioration can be traced to a place beyond the developments of suburban Washington, beyond the smokestacks of Baltimore, all the way north to the farms of Pennsylvania and New York. Because of this, she wanted Bjerke to see the bay, to learn what it has become, and to that end she had provided him and twenty others from the Department of Agriculture with a day she hoped they wouldn't forget.

They had spent hours on a boat, learning about critical habitat while floating on water that stretched as far as the eye could see. They had caught crabs, hundreds of them, and they had dredged up dozens of oysters that, split open right there on deck, tasted as good as any oyster ever has. They had seen herons and ospreys, egrets and ducks, and they'd had a dinner that featured cold, cold beer and far more fresh crabs than anyone could ever eat. And now the sun was down, and Bjerke was out on the dock, looking.

Somewhere to the north, well beyond the horizon, the runoff from thousands of farms was moving down the Susquehanna River. Meanwhile, the Potomac River was swollen, as always, with the treated sewage of several million people, and, to the south, the James River was taking on its usual doses of industrial discharges that include heavy metals such as lead and zinc. All of this, and more, was heading into the bay, as it does all the time, every day.

On Port Isobel, however, lovely and isolated Port Isobel, Bjerke stood on the dock, gazing out at the gentle green water, and said of the bay, "Looks good to me."

Now, here came the moon, a white crescent rising into the purple sky.

"Isn't this a perfect evening?"

* * *

It was, which underscores the central paradox of the Chesapeake Bay: It is a contradiction, a blending of beauty and decay, and because of that no one knows how it's doing. There are people who say they do know, that the bay is dying, that in some places it's already dead. But they really don't know, not entirely. They can't. It's too big. There's too much to understand. It is 195 miles long. It has 1,750 miles of navigable shoreline. It contains 18 *trillion* gallons of water, water that once was thought to flush directly into the Atlantic but now is known to wash this way and that, first south, then north, again and again before reaching the ocean, a process that allows much of the sediment and pollution to settle onto the bay's bottom. It took years for scientists to learn just that one basic dynamic of the bay, so how could any one person understand it all?

And yet, every day, any number of people continue to try. Currently, there are eight federal agencies involved in studying the bay, plus agencies from Maryland, Virginia, Pennsylvania and the District of Columbia. Plus universities. Plus legislatures. Plus environmental groups. All with their own agendas, their own methods, their own conclusions.

There is the Alliance for the Chesapeake Bay. "We hope we're holding the line," is Frances Flanigan's opinion. "There are some signs the bay is getting better in certain areas, but it would be wrong to say the bay is rebounding, because it's not yet."

There is the Environmental Protection Agency's special Chesapeake Bay office, which is busy these days generating computerized simulations of the bay that will help guide restoration efforts into the next century. "The bay is not in good shape," Charles Spooner, deputy director of the office, says of what the data from dozens of monitoring stations is showing. "The human analogy is we're all dying. Some days are better than others."

There is the Chesapeake Bay Foundation, the best known of the advocacy groups, which has 82,000 dues-paying members, 125 employees, a $7 million budget and, according to Rod Coggin, the public relations director, "seventeen education-research vessels — and that doesn't include three mobile canoe fleets." On any given day, the boats are out on the bay, filled with schoolchildren, as many as 30,000 a year, all learning that the bay is sick, the bay is on the brink, the bay needs help. In addition, the foundation has a mailing list of nearly 2 million homes, which recently received a fund-raising letter that began, "Dear Friend of the Bay, The Chesapeake Bay is still *dying*."

Is it really, though?

"In the strict biological sense, it isn't. In the sense of what we value, it is," says Tom Horton, a former Chesapeake Bay Foundation staff member whose recently completed assessment of the bay, *Turning the Tide*, was published in 1991.

"It's not dying. There is life. An algae bloom is life. But the species people care about have been going downhill, and so has the water quality," says Cindy Dunn, a field officer of the Alliance for the Chesapeake Bay, who is visiting with Horton on a recent afternoon.

"You could keep a room full of scientists debating a long time over whether the bay is producing any less life than it did fifty years ago," says Horton.

"I think it's safe to say it's declining," says Dunn.

"Changing," says Horton.

Why, then, is it so frequently described as dying?

"To raise money," Horton says, laughing.

"It's hard to get people's attention," says Dunn. "If you said the bay is suffering from eutrophication, you've just glazed over your public."

In any case, the attention-seeking has worked. It is said no bay in America has been studied as much as the Chesapeake, beginning with a report by the Environmental Protection Agency in 1983 that said fish, waterfowl and plant life in the nation's most productive estuary had declined to critical levels. Perhaps the attention is because the bay's proximity to Washington makes it a convenient environmental symbol. Or perhaps it's because, as bays go, the Chesapeake truly is extraordinary. This has been known for centuries, of course, but over the past few decades the appreciation has moved from lyricism to science.

At first, the bay was studied narrowly, with the focus on its changing water quality, but more recently it has been regarded as the victim of a far greater change, of the excesses of progress, and the focus has broadened to include its whole watershed, the area whose waters are received by the bay. The watershed of the Chesapeake is enormous. It is where more than 13 million people live. It covers 64,000 square miles spread over six states and the District of Columbia, and everything that leaches through the ground into its aquifers or drains into its hundreds of creeks, streams and rivers eventually ends up in the bay. The sewage. The industrial discharges. The pesticides applied to lawns. The herbicides applied to gardens and golf courses. The residues that are flushed from roadways in rainstorms. The rainwater itself, which we have come to realize is less pure than we once imagined. Making all of this worse is the fact that the bay is significantly shallower than most coastal bays, which means there is less water to absorb what comes its way.

There is one other essential fact about the bay: Over years of study, the realization has emerged that it has been altered less by lethal poisons than by the basic nutrients that cause plants to grow. Every water sample pulled out of the Chesapeake these days confirms that there is too much phosphorus and too much nitrogen in the bay. There is, in other words, an overabundance of nutrients, too much of a necessary thing, and one result of that is uncontrolled algae blooms, which turn the water opaque, which keeps out the sunlight, which causes the underwater grasses to die, the very grasses where fish spawn and crabs linger and life for the bay has been centered.

Now, says Horton, the center of bay life has shifted more toward the middle and surface areas. On the bottom, the number of oysters has declined to 1 percent of what was there several decades ago, while in the middle and on top roam bigger and bigger gangs of plankton. "I guess we could quibble forever over whether it's dying," Horton says of the bay, "but it's not what it used to be."

Still, there seems to be no shortage of crabs. Underwater grasses are said to be making a comeback. Rockfish too. And perhaps even oysters, which were found alive and healthy this winter in a few places where they haven't been found that way in years. So on one hand the bay is declining. But on the other it seems to be doing well.

So you can go to Baltimore and watch the dredges bring up the bottom of the harbor, a black mayonnaise that when exposed to fresh air turns a nauseating shade of gray.

Or you can go to Bloodsworth Island and see one of the largest, and most unusual, great blue heron rookeries in the East.

Located in waters just north of the Maryland-Virginia line, the island is 6,000 acres of uninhabited marsh whose defining feature, other than its heron nests, is thousands of craters caused by Navy bombs. "It's used daily between 9:00 A.M. and 4:00 P.M. from February through October," says Jim Brantley, a spokesman for the Navy, which has been bombing the island since 1942. "It's used mostly by planes, and they drop inert bombs. It's a bomb that doesn't really explode that much. It's a target-type bomb rather than a damage bomb."

That's now. In the past, the bombing runs included napalm, which set parts of the island on fire, burning up the pines and oaks that the herons used for nests. To fix what it had destroyed, the Navy later put up twenty or so specially built nesting towers, each consisting of a tall pole with several levels of platforms, almost all of which are now being used. And that is the contradiction of Bloodsworth. On an island that has decayed from its use as a bombing range, the great blue herons are nonetheless thriving. "Well, it's complicated," Tom Horton says about this. "What it says is you can't make simple assumptions."

* * *

It is complicated, with layers so wide and deep and linked that the way to best understand the complexities of the bay is to look at some of its problems. The developments. The runoff. The cows.

One of the bay's biggest problems, for instance, turns out to be Lancaster County, Pennsylvania, where, to the bay's detriment, the cows can't stop going to the bathroom. There are 100,000 dairy cows in the county, each of which produces about 120 pounds of manure a day. "When you think about it, you think, 'My God! How could she produce so much?'" says Gerald Heistand, of the Lancaster County soil conservation office. "But when you're shoveling it, you think, 'My God! She does!'"

And that's only the beginning. When you add up the amount of manure produced by all the farm animals of the county, the total exceeds 30 million pounds a day. Or 11 *billion* pounds a year. And all of it is rich in nitrogen and phosphorus, which leaches into the county's creeks and streams, which drain into the Susquehanna River, the dominant tributary of the bay.

If you look at a typical map of the Chesapeake, that won't be evident. There is Virginia on one side, Maryland and Delaware on the other, the Atlantic on the bottom right and the bay in between, long and spiny and always reassuringly blue. If you look closely at the top, however, you'll see one other bit of blue between the Maryland towns of Perryville and Havre de Grace, a skinny, unimportant-looking stripe that seems to peter out in the amorphousness of lower Pennsylvania. That is the Susquehanna. It is actually a wide, fast-flowing river that runs through Pennsylvania top to bottom and, according to a forty-year flow average, adds 25 billion gallons of water to the Chesapeake a day. It is said to be the source of half of the fresh water in the bay. It is also said to be the source of half of the phosphorus and three-fourths of the nitrogen in the upper part of the bay, the part above the Potomac. And the cows of Lancaster County are said to be one of the main reasons why.

The farmers of Lancaster County don't entirely believe this. "In our mind, it is not a big problem," says one farmer, Clyde Kreider. However they also know what their cows can do. "They go to the bathroom *everywhere,*" says Sue Zeidler, a worker on creeks, but Lancaster is thought to contribute the most. And so, with limited success, Gerald Heistand, of the county's conservation office, has taken on the job of educating farmers about the faraway bay. He tries offering dire warnings: The excess nitrogen not only hurts the bay, but, closer to home, it can contaminate well water with unsafe levels of nitrates. He tries offering money: If a farmer agrees to adopt management practices to control erosion and runoff — for instance, fencing off creeks to keep out the cows — the federal government has a program to pay at least half of the costs.

That program has been voluntary. So far, of the thousands of farmers in the county, 144 have signed on, and nine more are thinking it over, and that has been the extent of the response to Gerald Heistand.

"Some people don't believe it. They think it's a hoax," is Heistand's explanation for a farmer's reluctance to believe he has an effect on the bay.

"Yeah, but they don't know quite everything, either," is how Doris Landis reacts to explanations such as that.

There is nothing impolite in her tone, only a suggestion of weariness. She and her husband have been up since dawn, tending to the demands of their farm. They have 300 acres of corn and alfalfa, all of it to provide food for the cows. There are the fields to tend to, and there are the cows themselves. At the moment, the count is 260. Soon all of them will have to be milked for the third time this day. Not to mention fed. And the little bulldozer awaits.

* * *

Meanwhile, in the greater Washington metropolitan area, the problem for the bay is that the humans are behaving like cows. The humans, however, have an advantage. Instead of cropland, they have the Blue Plains Wastewater Treatment Plant as an intermediary between themselves and the bay.

Put simply, there are few places anywhere like Blue Plains. "We have tour groups from all over the world," says Ed Scott, acting administrator of the facility. "Russians have been here. Germans. Czechs. When you go to national conferences, international conferences, everyone knows Blue Plains." Its nickname? The "Craphouse Taj Mahal." It's a nickname of some respect.

And what exactly does Blue Plains do to earn such respect? It takes the raw sewage of more than 2 million people and cleans it so thoroughly that when it is finally dumped into the Potomac, it is glass-clear and relatively phosphorus-free. Blue Plains serves as a constant reminder that the health of the Chesapeake is dependent not only on what's already there but also on what is coming its way. Just as this applies to the Susquehanna, it applies to the Potomac, which dumps an average of 9 billion gallons of water into the Chesapeake a day. It is the bay's second-biggest tributary. It too carries a lot of agricultural runoff down from its upper reaches, but the addition of wastewater, at least wastewater the way it used to be treated, is what, for a time, made it a symbol of urban, environmental decay. That was in the 1960s. Then Blue Plains was upgraded at a cost that will exceed a billion dollars when all the improvements and expansions are done in a few years. Now, while the Potomac is hardly pristine, neither is it as bad as it was. It is fished everywhere, even at the exact point where the treated sewage of Blue Plains enters the river. And while the nitrogen levels in the treated sewage remain high, the phosphorus levels have been reduced significantly. Twenty years ago, Blue Plains was adding more than 6 million pounds of phosphorus a year to the Potomac and, by extension, to the bay. Now, after improvements, the number is down to 75,000 pounds, which is about as low as it can get.

The results of this are that the algae blooms of the Potomac have been reduced, and the Chesapeake has been given something of a break. And Blue Plains, along with an area wide ban on phosphates in laundry detergents, gets much of the credit. It has had its problems over the years, including a few battles with the EPA over treatment consistency, but when the plant is running smoothly, its capabilities can seem remarkable.

Its size too. It covers 154 acres in far Southeast Washington and handles about 70 percent of the sewage from the metropolitan Washington area, or about 310 million gallons a day.

Inbound sewage is funneled into Blue Plains through four huge, rectangular pipes, each twelve feet high and fifteen feet wide. From those pipes, the sewage moves into a series of pools for the first stage of treatment, a general straining through a line of vertical, metal bars. It is at this point that the untreated sewage can first be seen. "It's 99 percent water," says Walter Bailey, chief of the plant's wastewater division, explaining why it doesn't look as bad as might be expected. He is standing on a walkway, looking down at the wastewater as it approaches the bars. The view is of gray, opaque liquid, and several pieces of wood, and at the far end, moving around in lazy circles, a blur of white. Could it be a fish?

"That's a condom," Bailey says. "We get thousands and thousands of them. What'd you think happened to them?" Nonchalantly, he watches it move toward the bars. "You see all kinds of objects," he says and is happy to list them. Sticks. Bottles. Cans. Big pieces of plastic. Occasionally, a small animal. Infrequently, a human limb. Every so often, a fetus. "We've had to call the police two or three times." And cash, he says, lots of cash. "One of our operators found $1,500 not too long ago, rolled up in a rubber band."

All of this comes into Blue Plains, which makes what goes out that much more incredible. After passing through the bars, the sewage moves into a network of long, slow-flowing pools where the phosphorus removal begins. This is done with the help of what is called waste pickle liquor, a greenish-looking liquid that is a byproduct of the Bethlehem Steel plant outside Baltimore. The pickle liquor comes to Blue Plains by truck, ten trucks a day, each truck containing 4,000 gallons. In a never-ending shower, it is dumped onto the never-ending flow of sewage. It attaches itself to the phosphorus particles, and the particles become so heavy that they sink and can be easily removed as the sewage moves along its route.

Next stop for the sewage: primary treatment, where a mechanical scraping arm pivots around a giant, cylindrical holding tank, and 50,000 pounds of phosphorus settles out a day. Then: secondary treatment, where another 50,000 pounds is removed. Also in secondary treatment, in addition to more pickle liquor being added, the sewage is attacked by microorganisms that feast on the very things that would otherwise turn the Potomac back into the mess it was. These things are flocks of fats, proteins and carbohydrates. If they reached the river, they would decompose. Their decomposition, in turn, would attract microorganisms that live in the river and are always on the prowl for food. The microorganisms would eat like kings, but in the process of metabolizing their food they would use up the river's oxygen. And with that, the river would suffocate. Thus the need for secondary treatment. Instead of doing it in the river, the microorganisms do their eating in the tanks of Blue Plains.

At this point, the treatment regimen of most sewage-treatment plants would be completed. Not at the Taj Mahal, though. After secondary treatment, the wastewater is attacked by more microorganisms that convert the nitrogen content into a form that won't be toxic to fish. Then the microorganisms are removed. Then the wastewater is treated with chlorine to kill the microorganisms that escaped removal. And treated with sulfur dioxide to convert the chlorine, which would kill fish, into sodium chloride, which is salt. And aerated so it will be swollen with extra oxygen, which the fish will like. And filtered one more time, this time through sand and charcoal, to take out any remaining solids. And only then, 18 hours after its arrival through the big pipes of Blue Plains, is the wastewater pushed into the Potomac, no longer gray, no longer opaque and almost entirely phosphorus free.

Where is the phosphorus? It's in the 3 million pounds of sludge removed from the wastewater each day. Most of it gets trucked to farms in Virginia and Maryland, where it is applied to fields in amounts that, it is hoped, won't allow it to leach back into the ground, into the streams, into the rivers, into the bay. And the nitrogen? Still in the wastewater, it is on its way to the bay. The technology exists to take the nitrogen out, Walter Bailey says, but adding the equipment would cost at least $200 million, which means it won't be added anytime soon.

So huge is Blue Plains that a tour of it takes several hours. At one point in the early stages, when the marvel of the place is still unfolding, the giddy thought occurs that civilization is an amazing thing. Later, at the end of the tour, after all of the pools and ponds have blurred into one giant, 300-million-gallon morass, the thought changes somewhat: Civilization, above all, is a messy thing.

That, of course, is why Blue Plains exists, but also why, as successful as it has been, it will ultimately prove inadequate. It can only do so much. Any technology has its limits. Currently, Blue Plains is puffing along at capacity. An expansion underway on the site's few unused acres will increase the capacity by about 60 million gallons a day. But according to population projections, which can be extrapolated quite easily into sewage projections, the new, improved capacity will be reached in 20 years. At that point, another expansion will be needed, but not at Blue Plains, which will be forever out of room.

What happens then? Bailey shrugs and gives a look not unlike the one he gave the condom.

"We know we have capacity for twenty years," he says. "After that, it gets very difficult to predict."

* * *

Meanwhile, on Tilghman Island, the problem for the bay is that the humans are behaving like humans. And that might be the biggest problem of all.

"All right! It's the Ladies' Best Buns Contest!" Buddy Harrison hollers to the beery crowd assembled outside his hotel, Harrison's Chesapeake House. "Who's gonna be the lucky lady?"

It is Memorial Day, and on Tilghman, an island on Maryland's Eastern Shore, Harrison's parking lot is filled. Mostly, the crowd is from the Eastern Shore region, but not entirely. There's a Mercedes from Delaware, a Miata from Pennsylvania, and, out back, down by the water, there's a woman calling herself Niki who is rumored to be from somewhere around D.C. She is up on a second-floor balcony of the hotel, dancing for the crowd. Two other women, her competitors, are also dancing up there. They are both from the Eastern Shore, as different from Niki as can be. Both of them have what appear to be tattoos, for instance, and Niki, it will become apparent, does not.

There are many ways to view Niki, and one of them is symbolically, as one more outsider attracted to the bay. It has been estimated that as many as 3 million people will move into the Chesapeake watershed in the next 30 years. The ripple effects on the Chesapeake itself are predictable — more houses, which means less forest; more boats, which means more fishermen; more cars, which means more people going to places where they haven't gone before. On Tilghman Island, population 850, the process has already begun. At the drawbridge linking Tilghman to the mainland, the lines are only getting longer. And on the island itself, just past Harrison's hotel, two men, both involved in a waterfront real-estate project that will change life on the island irrevocably, are having a conversation about what is heading their way.

"It's coming," says David Bowen, a realtor. "People are moving in, displacing the watermen."

"No, we're *not* displacing the watermen. Don't *say* that," says Bill Davis, sales manager for the project, called Tilghman-On-Chesapeake. "That's why I helped put eight of their boats in last night, so they wouldn't think that."

"That's the way *they* feel, though," Bowen says.

"Yeah," Davis concedes, "it is."

In fact, they do. There is nothing new in this; for years stories have detailed woe upon woe of the Chesapeake watermen, including the notion that development is crowding them out. It's happened at Annapolis, at Rock Hall, at Solomons, at Oxford... The stories are so frequent they blur together sometimes. But that doesn't mean they're not true. Just up the road from Tilghman Island is the example of St. Michaels, which has been transformed from a scruffy watermen's hole into a precious cluster of gift shops and boutiques. Until the arrival of Tilghman-On-Chesapeake, though, the transformations stopped there. Past the last boutique, the landscape returned to large swaths of wilderness, miles of wilderness until Tilghman, which, in contrast to St. Michaels, seemed especially rough and authentic. Drive onto Tilghman, and you see: plain houses. Two old Methodist churches. The volunteer fire department. A small school. A lot of fishing boats, including some skipjacks, the big wooden dredging boats that used to fill the bay. A cemetery. Farms. And a dock, which, like Niki, turns out to be another symbol of Tilghman's transformation.

Decades ago, toward the turn of the century, the end of the dock was a steamboat pier. That was when the Eastern Shore was largely disconnected from the rest of the world and the bay was filled with what seemed like limitless oysters and fish.

Then it became the site of the Tilghman Packing Co. "We used to process oysters, clams, shad, herring, corn and tomatoes," says Buddy Harrison, whose family owned the land and the packinghouse. "We did things wrong, but we didn't know any better. We caught too many fish. We'd let the juices from the tomato processing run straight overboard, and that caused problems. There were times it would turn the sides of the houses on the water black, it was so acidic." And abundant. Not only the tomatoes but everything. The oysters, Harrison remembers, were shucked, packaged and sent out by the hundreds of thousands. The herring were pickled and shipped by the millions. There was so much work that the plant had hundreds of employees, nearly everyone on the island who wasn't a full-time fisherman.

Now? The packinghouse is gone. As the oysters and fish declined, it did too, until it finally went out of business. The Harrison family sold the land to someone who sold it to someone else, who sold it to some Columbia developers, who are developing Tilghman-On-Chesapeake. They own the dock and a swatch of land along the water that has been divided into lots. Such is the interest in protecting the Chesapeake these days that they had to get approval for the development from 18 federal, state and county agencies. It took months, but now the end of the dock is under construction for the third time in its existence. Now it will be a clubhouse.

With a pool. And a view of 114 deep-water boat slips and seventy-three home sites whose prices — just for the lot, not including a house, not including a slip — range from $69,000 to $250,000. "It may sound high," Bill Davis says, "but $60,000 in St. Michaels buys you a little quarter-acre lot, and you don't know where the water is."

He is standing at the end of the dock when he says this, looking back at the cleared acreage where the first house is being built. The dock is close enough to Buddy Harrison's hotel that Davis can hear the commotion, but he is focused on the vision of seventy-three homes. They'll be nice, he says, and even though the new residents will increase the island's population by 25 percent, their ripples will be hardly felt. So far, only one lot has been sold, but, with a salesman's confidence, Davis says it's only a matter of time. "They'll sell," he says. "It's going to happen whether we do it or not."

Over at Harrison's, the focus is a simpler one: enjoying a few hours by the bay. There's loud music and a lot of beer and a crowded dock where a woman, dangling one of her feet over the edge, drops her sandal by mistake into the water. Her husband sighs and goes to get it. He is about to get to know the bay intimately. He walks from the dock onto the shore, which is covered with plastic cups and cigarette butts and oil rainbows from boats. He takes a step into the water and sinks into muck. He grabs the sandal and tosses it to his wife, but it comes in low, hits the side of the dock and drops into deeper water. Now he's a little angry. He goes after it, sinks farther, up to his ankles, past his ankles, loses his balance, falls. He grabs the sandal, heaves it hard toward his wife, climbs out of the muck and water and stalks off. His wife watches him go. "He's a hosehead," she says. "This is the part he wanted to see too."

She means the contest. The crowd turns away from the bay to watch. The two locals may have their tattoos, but Niki has brought a tote bag containing high heels and a scarf. No doubt about this one. The outsider wins.

* * *

In the middle of the bay drifts a boat. It is a Chesapeake Bay Foundation boat, and on it are twenty-five high school students from Baltimore, most of whom have never seen the bay beyond Baltimore's Inner Harbor. They don't know about Lancaster County or Blue Plains or Tilghman Island. They don't know much of anything about the bay at all. The thing is, there are any number of ways to look at the bay, any number of parts that could be examined in addition to shoreline development, or cow manure, or human waste. In the Elizabeth River, fish were showing up for a while covered with tumors and cataracts; in Baltimore, the outer harbor has been showing signs that it may be overcoming decades of poisoning; in the main channel, measurements indicate the level of the bay may be slightly on the rise. There is the troubling decline in the variety of waterfowl population. There is the cautionary note about the crab population, that even though as many as ever are being caught, it is taking a larger number of crabbers to do it. There are the problems of industrial discharges and pesticide use, of city-street runoff and declining forest lands, of air pollution and acid rain. What the students know of the bay, though, is only what they are seeing, which is more water than most of them have ever seen before.

"If everybody looks as far north as they can see, as far east as they can see, as far south as they can see, and as far west as they can see, I know that you're probably looking at 8 to 10 percent of the entire bay. That's how big it is," their guide, Lou Etgen, tells them. "The bay is huge. We don't need to worry about a thing, right?"

He tells them why they do. He tells them about the grasses that maybe are coming back, and the oysters that maybe aren't. He mentions the watershed and the 13 million people, the farms and sewage, the nitrogen and phosphorus, the shad and rockfish, and then he gives them time to look around.

They are slightly south of the Bay Bridge at this point, on a patch of water that probably came into the bay from the Susquehanna, water whose temperature at the surface is about 70 degrees, whose clarity allows less than three feet of visibility, whose salinity level is in the medium range, whose dissolved oxygen level is in the low range but not dangerous. That's one way to look at the bay, but the other way is to do what the students are doing, to enjoy the moment, to just look. The day is beautiful. The water is beautiful. The boat's engine is off.

The bay is absolutely quiet, which gives the moment a timeless quality, a sensation not only of drifting on water but of being suspended in the middle of something infinite and wonderful, of floating.

"What do you think?" Etgen asks after a while.

"It's dying?" asks one student.

"It doesn't look bad to me," says another.

"That's the problem," Etgen says. He tells them the water used to be so clear that a person could stand in it up to his chin and be able to see his toes. Now the water's not clear, and neither is anything else.

MODERN MAN

Bill Gifford

THE STORY OF THE OYSTER has been one long decline. "We have wasted our inheritance by improvidence and mismanagement and blind confidence," mourned the great oyster biologist William Brooks in his 1891 treatise *The Oyster*. Chesapeake oysters are now so scarce that the organizers of a recent Talbot County waterfowl festival resorted to serving oysters from the Gulf of Mexico. They turned out to be bad, sending dozens of attendees to local hospitals in the throes of digestive mayhem.

How did it come to this, when the great-great-great-grandchildren of a single, healthy, female *Crassostrea virginica* would equal the volume of the planet Neptune, if they all survived? Seneca put his finger on part of the problem: the oyster's way of exciting, rather than sating, human appetites. Pollution also contributed. At the perilous intersection of human commerce and the ecology of the bay, the oyster became road kill.

Now nature is stepping in to finish the job man started, with two mysterious but deadly (to oysters) diseases. The result is not only a biological crisis — oysters are thought to be the ecological linchpin of the bay — but a cultural one as well. We may yet witness the disappearance of an iconic American food, a victim of scarcity and changing eating habits.

"The oyster," marveled M.F.K. Fisher, "leads a dreadful but exciting life." This is not necessarily true of all oysters — some, as we shall see, are coddled almost from birth — but it is for the particular oyster I have in mind. I met this oyster, in fact, at one of the most dreadful moments of its three-year life. It had been ripped from its home on the bottom of Chesapeake Bay and deposited on the culling ramp of a boat called the *Joan II* one sunny morning in mid-November. A young waterman named Lee Hickman plucked it from a muddy heap of similarly doomed oysters. With a few expert chops of an iron hatchet, he hacked it clean of mussels and barnacles and other unmarketable marine life and tossed it over to me, saying, "See where it attached itself?"

I held the oyster in my hand and saw how its hinge was fused to a fragment of another oyster's shell, still damp and filmed with silt. It was an unexceptional oyster, just over the legal market length of three inches. Yet it was remarkable, in the way any oyster is remarkable. It had, I was fairly certain, quite a tale to tell.

That it achieved adulthood at all represents a triumph against huge odds. The trouble began with the sex life of its parents, which was, to put it frankly, orgiastic. Both parents were equally irresponsible. The warming of the water in late spring is what got things going: Her dormant urges awakened, the mother trickled forth eggs by the millions, while her male neighbors surrendered their sperm in quantities that Brooks found "great beyond all powers of expression."

This went on for several days (no oyster is inhibited by anything resembling a brain), leaving both parents, but especially the male, utterly spent. The male cloud swirled and eddied about the female cloud. The union produced a million or so of the barely visible specks of oyster called "spat," which propelled themselves by means of a rudderlike foot.

My oyster took advantage of this, the only freedom it would ever know, in a characteristically youthful way: by wasting it. Completely lacking ambition, it swam in idle circles, allowing the tides to sweep it to and fro as most of its tiny siblings were killed — eaten usually. So who could blame my oyster for deciding, at the age of about two weeks, to settle down?

So down it settled, literally, drifting toward the bottom with its rudimentary foot extended, seeking some hard surface upon which to make its home: a wooden piling, a rusty anchor, even an old leather boot would do. Anything but the soft Chesapeake mud, which smothered still more of its hapless siblings. Luckily, it alighted upon another oyster's shell, the classiest, most desirable sort of oyster real estate. Layer by layer, it grew a shell as unique as a human footprint. When the tide ran, it opened the shell to strain nourishment from the life-giving water. When it sensed danger approaching, a rockfish or perhaps a crab, it clamped shut with a single strong muscle. It was perfectly satisfied with its new home, and settled in for a life of dull prosperity. My oyster acquired an identity of its own, became unmistakably a *Crassostrea virginica*, akin to but distinct from the Japanese-origin *gigas* oysters farmed on the West Coast and the platelike *Ostrea edulis* found seaweed-wrapped in Paris market stalls. It also could not be mistaken for the *virginica* native to Long Island Sound or Apalachicola Bay or even Chincoteague Bay.

Sequestered on the cold, dark bottom of the bay, my oyster concerned itself only with piling on layers of shell and spawning, ecstatically, once a year. Yet so much depended upon it: Rockfish and crabs tried to make it their dinner; small darting fish used it for cover; mussels and barnacles hitched themselves to its shell. It occupied a key link in the food chain, straining microscopic plants from the water and converting them into something recognizable as meat.

"They're probably the most important animal in the bay, ecologically speaking," says William Goldsborough, a fisheries biologist with the Chesapeake Bay Foundation.

The oyster's influence extended well beyond the water's edge. Towns were named in its honor: Bivalve, Maryland, and Oyster, Virginia, are just two. Every fall, a flotilla of boats set forth to pursue it, while a small army of shuckers and boat builders and truck drivers wait on land. Trees died that the oyster might live, but all the studies, laws and newspaper editorials printed over the last century and a half have failed to halt its inexorable decline.

* * *

My oyster's forebears were good, though not overly, to one fellow in particular, a hulking Kent Island waterman named Joe Coleman. They helped to pay for his house on Benton's Pleasure Road in Chester, his new Nikes, and his boat, the thirty-five-foot *Joan II*, which on this November morning is fighting a strong Kent Narrows tide.

Right now, Coleman's mind is not on the fickle oyster but on the *Joan II*'s aging engine. He mistrusts the temperature gauge mounted inside the pilothouse, so he sends his partner, Chris Kayhoe, aft with a flashlight. Kayhoe and their crewman, Hickman, heave aside the engine cover and peer into the dark, roaring cavity. "One-eighty," Kayhoe reports. Coleman grimaces.

A few minutes later, he sends Kayhoe back again. Still 180 degrees. Having cleared the worst of the tide, Coleman throttles back and relaxes a bit. In the pre-dawn darkness, through the moisture condensing on the windowpanes, I can discern the silhouette of a channel marker and the running lights of half a dozen vessels, and still more are trailing behind. As the procession swings north into the wide Chester River, Kayhoe lights his fourth cigarette of the day. Coleman looks pained; he quit seven years ago. "This is a nonsmoking section," he protests.

Born on Kent Island fifty-seven years ago, Coleman moved away as a boy — all the way to Grasonville, just across the Narrows. His chest and arms are powerful from years of hoisting heavy iron tongs, which is how Coleman gathered oysters before he met Kayhoe. Because of his size, folks around the docks know him as "Captain Bull Moose." His son, Wade, a collegiate discus thrower, has shown no desire to follow his father. "He wants to be a schoolteacher," Coleman tells me, incredulous.

Although Kayhoe is a familiar figure around Kent Narrows, the stocky 34-year-old is anything but a traditional waterman. He grew up in Kensington, the son of a physician, and attended Good Counsel High School. In a community of pickup trucks, he drives a white Volvo with a car phone. Kayhoe is an oyster diver, a modern breed of waterman. He started diving as a teenager, following his older brothers Rick and Doug into the water. He dove oysters as a student at the University of Maryland, then moved over to the Eastern Shore with his brothers.

Twenty years ago, there were only three ways to take oysters: by hand tongs, by hydraulic tongs or by skipjacks that dredged under sail power as required by an 1865 Maryland law. Each method has its advantages, but all are antiquated. In the mid-1970s, Rick Kayhoe was diving for a Bowie salvage firm, retrieving scrap metal from offshore wrecks, when he and a partner petitioned the Maryland Department of Natural Resources for permission to dive oysters commercially. State law did, after all, permit the gathering of shellfish "by hand."

"He wasn't local and neither was I," says Rick of his partner. "It was kinda the blind leading the blind. So we got some local boys to help us, they knew the bottom real good." Still, he says, "nobody thought you could make a living at it. You'd go into a bar and they'd buy you a drink and laugh at you. But in the winter, when we could send a diver through the ice, and work in worse weather — then it wasn't funny anymore. Then we were a viable threat to 'em."

If there's one thing a waterman detests, it's state restrictions. To his way of thinking, most of what comes out of Annapolis stops just short of communism. But when traditional hand-tongers saw divers gathering bigger oysters more quickly than they could, they experienced a quick conversion. At the tongers' behest, the state legislature passed a law banning divers from the best oyster grounds and imposing a minimum "keeper" size of four inches, rather than the usual three. A Queen Anne's County court nullified the size limit in 1983, and though some restrictions remain, oyster diving became lucrative.

The emergence of oyster diving is a function of the bivalve's decline. Tongs and dredges were ideal weapons with which to assail the towering oyster reefs or "rocks" that dotted the Bay in earlier years. Those are long gone. A diver can work today's sparse bars because he can see the oysters. A tonger might work the same bar from sunup to sundown and still fall short of his fifteen-bushel limit. Quite a few traditional watermen have enrolled in diving courses and now earn their living underwater rather than on its surface. Last year, divers accounted for one fifth of Maryland's oyster catch.

Chris is the only Kayhoe who still dives. Rick quit in 1985 with a sore back, and Doug developed carpal tunnel syndrome. Diving oysters in the bay is not particularly dangerous — divers rarely go deeper than about thirty feet — but neither is it completely safe. A few years ago, a diver got "hung up" on some underwater rubble and drowned. The oysters are collected in cages that are lowered with the divers, and a full cage can deliver a nasty blow when it is jerked away. For Kayhoe, each season is a running siege of sinus infections, sore throats and colds.

"Man wants to go diving," says Russell Dize, a Tilghman Island skipjack captain, "he deserves all the oysters he can get."

* * *

Coleman cuts the throttle back and we lie up by the left shore of the river. He'd rather not have the other boats follow him to the particular section he has in mind today. Once they've passed, we'll cross over to a hot spot another diver had told Kayhoe about, near some buoys. "It's a game of cat and mouse sometimes," Kayhoe says.

He takes the radio mouthpiece. "Hey, Bruce!" he calls.

"Gotcha back," the radio answers. "Where're them buoys?" Kayhoe asks. There is a pause. "There's a white one," Bruce says, "and a green one that's on toppa the mother lode."

Coleman snorts. "Probably the other way around."

"Or the other way round, I'm not sure," Bruce says. "You better check."

The airwaves crackle with cursing and laughter.

As the sun peers over the horizon, Coleman maneuvers the boat into position near a floating white bleach jug and heaves a wire cage over the side. Meanwhile, Kayhoe has stripped down to long johns and a Desert Storm sweat shirt, puffing furiously on one last cigarette. He pulls a thick rubber dry suit over his sweats, washes out his mask and mouthpiece, and hoists a heavy lead plate onto his back to weight him. Tossing out the cigarette, he pulls the mask over his face, swings his legs over the rail, and disappears feet first into the depths, trailing a yellow air hose.

Coleman works the throttle, maneuvering the boat to follow Kayhoe's bubbles. Hickman and I stand on deck. He's twenty-nine and rail-thin, slouching under a well-worn Maryland Watermen's Association cap. Hickman tells me he has his own boat, for crabbing. After crab season ends, he makes extra money culling for Coleman and Kayhoe. Just then, Hickman and I spot a string of migrating swans in the sky, several long V's of them beating down the flyway from the north. We watch them pass over Eastern Neck Island, their white bellies flashing the first rays of the sun, until Coleman begins hauling in the first cage and it's time to go to work.

* * *

Nearly half of Maryland's oyster harvest last year came out of the Chester, for the simple reason that it has largely escaped the two parasites, MSX and dermo, that have decimated oysters south of the Bay Bridge. Other rivers that once ranked among the bay's most productive, such as the lower Choptank, Wye and Nanticoke, are all but barren now. The Chester is too cold and too fresh for the parasites to take hold, which is why many of the state's working boats will be here today.

Most of the oysters they will harvest, mine included, were born not in the Chester but in the warmer, saltier, more amorous waters of Tangier Sound, about seventy-five miles to the south. There, oysters reproduce with abandon; in the chillier Chester, their ardor seems to wane. But had my oyster remained in its native Tangier, it almost certainly would have perished.

It was rescued one spring day in 1991 by a pair of metal tongs that scooped it off the bottom and deposited it, along with most of its neighbors, in a bushel basket. It was too small for market; rather it was being transplanted. As part of a $2 million oyster replenishment program, Maryland pays watermen to harvest baby oysters, called seed oysters, from fertile Tangier Sound and Kedges Strait and haul them north to the Chester River and a handful of other grounds — the upper bay, the upper Choptank and a Potomac River tributary called the Wicomico — where they are more likely to survive. The program is only a couple of decades old, but its roots reach back to the 1632 colony charter to Lord Calvert, which specified that Maryland's aquatic resources were to be utilized by the public and administered by the colony.

Without the intervention of the state, there would be no oyster fishery in Maryland. Under natural conditions, an oyster bar is self-perpetuating as spat alight on their elders' shells and grow. Commercial oystering initially expanded oyster habitat by breaking up the old reefs and strewing shell across a wide area of bottom. But ultimately the oyster harvest removed tons and tons of shell from the bay, shrinking the available habitat. The state now pays a contractor about $500,000 yearly to dredge shell from dead oyster bars and spread it on the spawning grounds of Tangier and Kedges, the better to collect the spat.

Habitat loss is a slow killer; MSX and dermo are more efficient. Neither is harmful to humans, but both are deadly to oysters, starving 90 percent of their victims within the three years it takes a bay oyster to reach market size. Dermo was first recorded in the Gulf of Mexico in the 1940s. MSX was identified in Delaware Bay in 1957, though some scientists believe it is what killed New England oysters in the 1930s. Both parasites converged on the bay in the early 1960s. They inflicted only modest damage until the drought years of the 1980s, when the salt-loving diseases exploded like twin depth charges.

Dermo is the deadlier of the two because the oyster cannot eliminate it; MSX, on the other hand, comes and goes. Dermo is pervasive in most of the bay's waters, but the low salinity of the upper bay tends to suppress it. Dermo is also epidemic in the Gulf, but the faster-growing warm water oysters can outrace the parasite, reaching market size in just a year or two. There is no known chemical treatment for dermo that does not also kill the oyster. Two scientists I spoke with likened it to Dutch elm disease. "We've got a biological war going on out there now," says W. Pete Jensen, director of fisheries for the Maryland Department of Natural Resources. "The parasites are evolving faster than the oysters."

The department may have aided the diseases. Dermo is thought to have been introduced to the Chester River via transplanted oysters. The low salinity keeps the parasites inactive, but a dry summer could change that. "We've moved disease," acknowledges one state official, "but we had reason to and watermen benefited from it."

Aside from its ecological benefits, the repletion effort amounts to a sort of jobs program for watermen. The state is spending $2 million to support a fishery that will yield about $1.4 million worth of oysters this year; six years ago, the state spent twice as much for 10 times as many oysters. Watermen pay a $300 license surcharge for the privilege of oystering, plus a dollar-a-bushel tax. But the returns for the 540 watermen who anted up the surcharge this year will be slim: less than $3,000 apiece.

* * *

Kayhoe swims to the boat and pulls himself up the ladder. After two hours, he looks exhausted, his eyes sunken and unfocused. Hickman lights him a Camel and hands it over, deftly sidestepping an irritated Coleman. "I'm not gonna stay out here for this," he says, flinging a shell at the piled-high cull ramp. "I oughta take a shovel and throw it overboard." The seed oysters are small and brittle, barely over market size. Earlier this morning, Kayhoe was gathering native Chester oysters, deep-cupped and heavy shelled. "If these are worth 20," Coleman says, waving toward the baskets of seed oysters, "these oughta be worth 50."

Coleman moves the boat to another spot, where he probes the bottom with a long wooden shaft. It sinks into mud. He moves again, and the shaft strikes something hard. Kayhoe finishes his cigarette and eases into the water. Baskets accumulate on the deck until 1:30, when Kayhoe has taken his and Coleman's limit of 30 bushels. Among divers, it's a matter of pride to "limit out" early; as we pass another boat where a friend of Kayhoe's is still working, Kayhoe pretends to slash his wrist mockingly.

Back at Kent Narrows, Coleman guides the *Joan II* to the dock of United Shellfish, where a workman loads the oysters onto a conveyor belt that deposits them in a mostly empty truck. Barry Schomborg, the chief buyer for United Shellfish, saunters out of his office and watches the oysters ride up the ramp, appraising them with a practiced eye.

Kayhoe follows him into the office, emerging a few minutes later with a wad of cash. Schomborg paid $17.50 a bushel, not bad for this season but half what a bushel might have brought 10 years ago, before a glut of cheap Gulf oysters depressed local prices. Kayhoe peels off four twenties for Hickman, and he and Coleman split the remainder, each grossing a little more than $200 for the day's work.

In three weeks, Kayhoe will drive up to Maine with some other local divers to gather sea urchins for the Japanese market. That brings a little more money, but it also means living in a motel for a few months. An enterprising man, Kayhoe earns the rest of his income peddling crabs and fish that other watermen have caught. On Saturdays through the summer and fall, he's most likely to be found at the farmers' market at RFK Stadium in Washington.

They like Kayhoe well enough down at the Kent Narrows slips, but, even after 15 years, he's not quite one of them. It's not because of the diving, or the Volvo either. "He's not a wooterman," says one older waterman finally, squinting across the bed of a pickup truck as his buddies nod agreement. "He's a businessman."

* * *

Sometime after the hand-tongers have unloaded their catch, the truck growls out of the United Shellfish lot and onto U.S. 301 South to deliver my oyster and a few thousand of its friends to the custody of Ronnie Bevans, the Chesapeake's oyster king. Should a Maryland oyster manage to survive disease, predation and myriad other potential misfortunes, the odds are excellent that it will end its life at Bevans's main shucking plant at Kinsale, in Virginia's Northern Neck.

A rural peninsula between the Potomac and Rappahannock rivers, the Northern Neck is a place of rolling fields, vine-choked farmhouses and small hamlets anchored by Baptist churches and farm supply stores. Most of all, though, it is a place defined by water, the broad Potomac and its coiling estuaries. Although Bevans Oyster Co. occupies a small promontory near the head of the Yeocomico River, most oysters arrive there by land in refrigerated cab-over trucks from Kent Narrows and Rock Hall, and huge, gleaming semitrailers hauling magnificent bluepoints from Long Island Sound and watery Gulf oysters from points south. It is a modest place, a small house surrounded by a few cinder block outbuildings and a small mountain of shells.

When Bevans went into business in 1966 there were "all the oysters you could buy," he says. "More than what you wanted, really." He had just eight employees then, including his wife, and everybody shucked. Now his three shucking houses employ 180 people at peak periods. But he has to scramble to find enough oysters for them to shuck. Each week during the fall and winter, as many as 3,000 bushels of oysters are unloaded here from up and down the East Coast. Most of his local competitors have gone out of business.

My oyster arrives in Kinsale at the height of the Thanksgiving rush, when Bevans's plants are shucking full tilt. It is unloaded and tossed into a steel hopper on an endless chain snaking from the loading dock into the low-ceilinged shucking room — where more than 60 shuckers are lined up at a sloping concrete counter. Each is equipped with an apron, rubber boots and heavy black gloves, plus a flat-bladed shucking knife. The shucking starts at 3:00 A.M., while the oysters are still fresh, and goes until ten or eleven o'clock.

A shucker needs more oysters, she reaches up and tips one of the hoppers. Not twenty-four hours after my oyster sat innocently on the bottom of the Chester, it is dumped onto the counter, seized by yet another gloved human hand, and most painfully violated.

Perhaps Eliza Henry does the deed — the 24-year veteran is among the house's faster shuckers. On another morning, she demonstrates her technique. Gripping a small oyster in her gloved left hand, she wedges the knife blade into its barely visible seam. Twisting the blade slightly, she pulls the oyster down, severing the adductor muscle. The shell opens, revealing white mantle.

"You move the oyster," she explains. "You never move the knife." I nod, wishing I'd known this before attempting to shuck oysters myself.

With a flick of the knife, she untethers the oyster from its home, and the gray oval of meat comes to rest in a stainless steel bucket. The shells skitter down a steep chute. Hefting the container, Henry guesses it will yield her about $9. Shuckers are paid a dollar a pound or minimum wage, whichever is greater, but few, if any, would work for minimum wage. Henry expects to make about $65 today. Tops for a good day is about 15 bucks more. "I've left to do other things," she says, "but I always come back. This is something it's not easy to stay away from."

In rural Westmoreland County, there are not many other employers. Fortunately for Henry and the other workers, nobody has yet invented a machine capable of shucking an oyster.

After the meat is weighed and the wage tickets are written, the oysters are poured into large steel canisters for rinsing and draining in a room fragrant with brine. There my oyster is entombed in a glass jar and trundled off that very day for points north, south and west. Three days or a week hence, it will appear in the seafood counter of some supermarket in Rapid City or maybe in an oyster stew served to a Las Vegas gambler.

* * *

If Coleman, Kayhoe and Hickman are hunters, then Bevans is a farmer. In addition to shucking and shipping other people's oysters, he plants his own, tending and harvesting them like underwater potatoes from the 8,000 acres of bottom that he leases from the state of Virginia. His domain extends from the U.S. 301 bridge over the Potomac all the way around to the James River spawning grounds, and includes parts of the Rappahannock, Great Wicomico and York rivers. This aquatic empire is delineated by marker buoys and wooden stakes and patrolled by radar-equipped boats and airplanes.

Dermo steals more of Bevans's oysters than poachers do, and it doesn't show up on radar. He vigilantly monitors the salinity of his grounds, and when it creeps too high, he pays local watermen to dredge up his oysters and replant them in safer water. By the time a Bevans oyster is shucked, it may have traveled extensively around Tidewater country.

It's no mystery why Bevans will produce ten times more oysters this year than watermen will take from public waters in Virginia and the Potomac: He owns those oysters. Therefore, he has a financial incentive to nurture each and every spat to adulthood. Maryland scientists have urged private oyster culture since William Brooks's day, but the idea has never really taken hold, largely due to the opposition of the state's watermen, who fear that a Ronnie Bevans will shove them aside.

"That's the thing we don't want to happen, one person monopolizing part of the Bay that 500 people could make a living off of," says Larry Simms, president of the Maryland Watermen's Association. "You'd take 500 individual businessmen and make them minimum wage laborers."

But public fisheries have their drawbacks too — chiefly, a dearth of oysters. Thousands of individual watermen have already become minimum wage laborers, working construction or in restaurants.

Brooks sized up the situation a century ago, his tongue firmly in cheek: "As the beds belong to the community, private oyster culture has not been permitted, since it would be a monopoly. Yet the common property of the citizen of the State has been given up to one class of citizens in order that they might have profitable employment. They have not managed their trust wisely, and have brought it so near the verge of ruin that it is no longer attractive to Marylanders."

The debate has raged since. Is it better to have one Ronnie Bevans with lots of oysters and hundreds of low-wage employees, or a few hundred Colemans and Kayhoes competing for an ever-dwindling resource?

Nature may resolve the question before politics does. However prolific the oyster may be, human appetites were not factored into its genetic equation. Wherever people have harvested oysters, from England and France to New England to the Pacific Coast, the pattern has been the same: The natural oysters are fished almost to death, only to return as farmed "product." The Ronnie Bevanses of the world — and the Eliza Henrys — have usually succeeded the Kayhoes and Colemans and Dizes.

For years Maryland policy was tilted toward public fishing, but now private oyster culture is being encouraged through an expanded leasing program. One afternoon, I drove to Pintail Point farm, on an arm of the Wye River. There I met Eric Powell, the resident aquaculturist. We drove past the farm's immaculate lawns, its cornfields, and the one-acre ponds where Powell raises striped bass. He showed me the long white tanks where baby oysters are raised, complete with nozzles and drains that precisely regulate the water flow over each oyster. Then we boarded a motorized raft and putted out to an array of about fifty small floats in midriver, wire mesh bins where oysters are matured. Powell bent down, removed the cover of one float and selected two identical oysters, each perfectly formed and unblemished by mussels or mud.

He pried one open with his knife, cracking the thin shell. The oyster looked fine, plump and clean, but when I popped it in my mouth, it was different; it lacked the familiar salty tang. We were so far up the Wye that the water was almost fresh; a half-mile downstream, in slightly saltier water, dermo has ravaged natural oyster beds.

On our way back to his office, Powell stopped near a wire duck enclosure. A tall man emerged, wearing hip-waders splattered with guano. "Donald!" Powell greeted him. "You're smelling *sweet!*" A grinning Donald Novak swaggered over to us, having just succeeded in herding Pintail Point's doomed ducks back into their cage for the night. The twenty-nine-year-old, it turns out, is a recently retired waterman. He went crabbing last spring, and planned to tong for oysters this fall, the way he had every season since high school, but over the summer, with three young children at home and the oyster more doubtful than ever, he put his boat on cinder blocks.

With every year of the oyster's decline, a certain number of watermen decide to quit and not come back, which gives the oyster a chance to recover. "Maybe it's nature's way," Novak said. "But let me put it this way: I'll always have my boat."

That afternoon at Pintail Point, I tasted the future of the American oyster, and it told me something about the fate of the bay and of the people who have earned a living from it for more than three centuries, and about what William Brooks called the blind confidence of humankind.

* * *

The Romans brought oysters home from their Anglo-Gallic outposts, while across the sea, Native Americans left behind shell piles of geological significance, the continent's first garbage dumps. Oysters were so plentiful that they seemed worthless. In 1680, one group of

Kent Island settlers complained of having to eat them, due to the scarcity of other food. George Washington fed them to his slaves. By the mid-19th century, when the French and English beds had been fished to extinction, the Chesapeake supply still seemed inexhaustible.

The European oyster was a noble delicacy — "the frond-lipped, brine-stung/glut of privilege," in the words of Irish poet Seamus Heaney. But the American version stuffed the streetcar conductor and the aristocrat alike. A 1918 pamphlet of the U.S. Department of Commerce touted oysters as "the food that has not 'gone up' [in price]," and suggested no fewer than a hundred ways to fix them: baked, fried, "panned" and grilled; in fritters, tartlets, shortcakes and potpies; and in such complicated concoctions as "veal-oyster frizee" and "oysters a la Newburg."

In recent years several well-publicized oyster-related deaths have inspired a backlash. Red Lobster quit serving raw oysters a few years ago. Food and Drug Administration Commissioner David Kessler advised consumers not to eat raw shellfish of any kind, and California, Louisiana and Florida require warning labels to be posted wherever raw oysters are served. Even the trade magazine Seafood Leader warned readers to avoid raw oysters.

But most likely, the ancestral memory of oyster-eating will persist. There will always be people willing to pay, say, $20 in a fine restaurant for half a dozen perfect specimens, nurtured from birth on the purest water and finest planktonic food, their growth and well-being monitored at every step, their shells absolutely unblemished, and their healthfulness certified by the relevant authorities. These oysters will be served on the half shell, displayed like fine jewels for the lucky few who will fork them down, then lean back and pronounce themselves quite sated, indeed.

PARADISE UNRECLAIMED

Tom Horton

PARRAMORE ISLAND, VIRGINIA — You could land jumbo jets on the expanse of white, packed sand beach here, stretching unpeopled for more than a dozen miles. Back of the dunes, the broad marshes are full of ducks and tangy salt oysters, and deer roam ancient forests of cedar and pine. This crown jewel of all the mid-Atlantic coast's bright string of sea islands, owned by a private nature trust and inaccessible to most people, seemed like paradise on a recent camping trip. We luxuriated in the thought about half a day before we began to rearrange paradise.

First, we scooped sand from the backside of a dune and propped old cedar logs around it to make a comfortable lean-to for shelter from the wind. Were we to be there much longer, we decided, we would chop one of the tall pines to bridge several of the island's deep marsh creeks for more convenient travel. A couple of creeks had barren, sandy bottoms, swept clean by the tides. There we would transplant a few beds of oysters from muddy locations, so they would grow better and be convenient to our campsite. A nearby high marsh, if diked, would make fine pasture for a few head of cattle, and for crops...and on and on the planning went, customizing the Garden of Eden.

The best of both worlds is what we seem really to crave. A little farm on Frazee Ridge with excellent schools and a large shopping center not too far away; trackless wilderness with a return each evening to a first-class hotel; and a sweeping view of unspoiled ocean coast in all directions — from the deck of our condominium. The best of both worlds, the natural and the manufactured — who could argue with the pursuit of that; and, by extension, with the extraordinary technological and economic progress that has enabled it? Even such a proponent of wilderness as Aldo Leopold had to concede that "wild things had little value until mechanization assured us of a good breakfast, and science disclosed the drama of where they come from and how they live."

The best of both worlds. It seems to imply an unalloyed good, but it also means there is a balance to be struck, and limits to our encroachment on the natural world of the Chesapeake region. To avoid facing this squarely is to risk bankrupting the Save the Bay movement that bids to become our environmental drumbeat through the remainder of this century. "Will we save the bay?" It is the question I am most asked since the landmark conference in 1983 when citizens, scientists, and their elected leaders met from across the watershed in Fairfax, Virginia, to discuss a six-year study documenting widespread and accelerating environmental declines in North America's greatest estuary.

I try to be optimistic. I tell people that since then we have committed more money and human resources to reversing the bay's downtrends than at any point in our history on its shores. It is nothing short of inspirational, I say, that on one of the bitterest weekends of winter nearly one thousand people in Pennsylvania, a state that owns not a square inch of the Chesapeake, braved icy roads and paid $10 each to attend a conference on how they could contribute to the bay's cleanup. Their concern is critical because, through its mighty Susquehanna River, Pennsylvania contributes not only half the fresh water of the Chesapeake Bay, but also enough pollution, mainly from its bountiful agriculture, that any meaningful cleanup of the bay will be literally impossible without a huge effort from the third of its watershed that lies in Pennsylvania.

I also tell people about more subtle, though no less important, moves afoot, such as the meeting one night to discuss pollution control between a concerned farmer from the Amish country in Lancaster County, and his counterpart from Virginia's tidewater, down on the Rappahannock — the two connected across 250 miles by a skein of water, flowing river at one's end, almost ocean at the other's; connected by their mutual caring about the whole of it.

I tell my questioners how we are upgrading the treatment of sewage to levels well beyond any legal requirements in some cases; also the controlling of sediment from land development, regulating even the polluted storm water that runs from the asphalt and concrete covering our communities; and recruiting small armies of technicians to help farmers keep their soil and chemicals on their land, instead of in our water. I recount how conservationists finally prevailed in 1984 in the bitterest natural-resources controversy in Maryland history since the Oyster Wars of the 1880s. They won a moratorium to stop all fishing for the troubled state fish, the rockfish, until we can once again make its spawning waters clean.

I note that where a problem — and its solution — can be defined, we are not grudging of money to pursue it. Baltimore's Back River was chosen a century ago as the dumping spot for the region's sewage, precisely because it had such poor flushing action that it would not let the wastes escape to the rest of the bay. The river became, in effect, the final stage of sewage treatment for the city; and many still feel that is a cost-effective strategy, especially because Back River never was the finest of waterways even in more pristine times. But citizens and government have overwhelmingly rejected that option, and we are preparing to spend a third of a billion dollars, maybe more, to upgrade the sewage-treatment plant in hopes of reclaiming Back River. Our sleaziest tributary, perhaps, but if money can buy it back, we'll take it, thank you.

Who could ever doubt that we want to save the bay? It is, after all, what makes this region, for so many of us, the best of both worlds. But having told people who would save the bay all of the above, I also caution them that the 1983 conference to save the bay was preceded by similar conferences in 1968 and in 1977. Like the third conference, the first two ended on hopeful and enthusiastic notes; indeed, the years following the first of those two gatherings witnessed the greatest surge of both federal and state anti-pollution legislation and spending in history, part of the dramatic rise of the modern environmental movement. I tell them what Bill Hargis, a long-time bay scientist, said of those years. We were making famous progress in fighting pollution, he said — moving upstream, with tremendous effort, at about three knots — only the current continued to run downstream at five knots. His point was that we do not perform our bay-saving in some laboratory where all parameters are under our precise control; we are not in a game where the forces of pollution take time out while we huddle on countermeasures. It is why, finally, I warn those who hope to save the bay that its epitaph has already been written, if not yet chiseled in stone.

There are a number of ways in which that proleptic epitaph can be stated, but I think it was particularly fitting the way it came from the mouth of a real-estate agent from the boom-growth bay-shore county of Anne Arundel. She was testifying against controversial new state legislation designed to limit the amount and the type of development of the most environmentally sensitive waterfront areas of the bay and its rivers. She feared this would affect her livelihood but also wanted the lawmakers to understand that it was as much in her interest as anyone's to want a healthy Chesapeake Bay: "We need the bay to stay clean and beautiful, so that people will continue to move here to enjoy it," she explained. Very nicely, and in all sincerity, she had defined the best of both worlds as we conceive it today in the Chesapeake region — that is, without limit on the number of those who would seek it, or on the share of the natural pie each would expect.

Irrevocably, and more than most bodies of water, our Chesapeake is "a people's bay," as William Ruckelshaus, director of the U.S. Environmental Protection Agency, called it at the 1983 conference; and therein lies both its infinite charm and the seeds of its destruction.

Compare the Chesapeake Bay to Puget Sound, San Francisco Bay, Delaware Bay — to almost any of the world's other great bays, gulfs, estuaries, and inland seas. You will be hard-pressed to find another where the water twines more extensively with the land in dozens of rivers and thousands of creeks; where the depths are as moderate, the tides as minimal, the seas as kindly, the bottoms as hazard-free, the seafood as abundant; where these and a dozen other factors, such as proximity to the nation's capital, conspire half so well to create water so eminently usable for so many purposes by such a large and growing population.

Our bay is a convivial bay, an accessible bay, a tasty bay. I know a single cove on a Talbot County tributary where the property owners harvest silver-kerneled sugar corn, tart and robust tomatoes, succulent canvasback duck and Canada goose, plump oysters the color of cream, sweet soft-shell crabs and firm-fleshed rockfish, as well as deer, coon, muskrat, quail, and rabbit; and a nearby poultry house grows Perdue Oven Stuffer Roasters! Such a cornucopia. I often decry Captain John Smith's over-quoted "heaven and earth never agreeing better for frame habitation for man" as a shameless bit of anthropocentrism — as if God and Ole Ma Nature had just been setting the table for fifteen thousand years or so in hopes that a crowd of unwashed Europeans would settle down for an extended free meal. But honestly, this bay and the ample regions it waters and drains do almost beg to be used.

And use it we have. Waterfront, waterview, water access, water privilege — nothing sells lots better than proximity to the shoreline. To the waterman, the bay is twenty-seven million pounds of oyster meats annually, and fifty-five million pounds of crab meat atop that. It is a vast and economical heat sink for power plants, the largest of which, Calvert Cliffs, sucks three billion gallons of bay water a day across its nuclear core to cool it. Our bay is highway and harbor to two of the world's greatest shipping complexes, at Norfolk and Baltimore; and the setting for millions of individual fishing and hunting trips each year. To the biologist it is a world class laboratory; to the industrialist and the sanitary engineer, an economical source of the dilution that once was considered the ultimate solution to pollution. It is a federal and a military bay, a proving ground for the big guns at Aberdeen, a bombing and strafing and shelling range for naval jets and destroyers at Bloodsworth Island; its depths are convenient to the Pentagon for underwater demolition experiments, which occasionally have blown up weakfish by the ton and oysters by the bar; and it is home port, near its mouth, to the U.S. Navy's Atlantic Fleet.

So many things the bay means to so many users, yet one thing it becomes for all of us — the ultimate sink, the settling basin, the end of the road, for sediment and chemicals and wastes that flow from our activities on the land; flowing from across a drainage basin that extends north as far as the New York Finger Lakes, south nearly into North Carolina, and west almost to Tennessee. The intimate connection between how we live on this land and the quality of the waters that drain it is a profound lesson we have learned belatedly; and with the knowledge has come almost agonizing recognition of a fundamental irony of public environmental policy toward the Chesapeake Bay: we hold its waters and their denizens to be a public trust, to be held in stewardship for future generations; while the surrounding land, most of the massive, 64,000-square-mile watershed, remains a free market commodity, its highest and best use largely determined by the short-term economics of individual gain. To the greater public interest, vested in state and federal government, has gone most of the rule over the water of the watershed; but land-use decisions remain the province of a thousand town and county governments, none of which wants its water to end up like Baltimore harbor, but most of which will fight to the death to retain the option to use its land just as intensively as the state's largest city, should the opportunity arise.

Grow or die is the watchword by which every political jurisdiction proceeds. Attract development. Increase the tax base. Stoke the economy. And of course, "Save the Bay" — no political platform would be complete without it. It is, after all, nothing less than the best of both worlds that we want, isn't it? The catch, of course, is that, even assuming the most technologically advanced and zealously enforced pollution controls (quite a big assumption), we are nowhere near the point where each additional resident does not constitute a net draft against the finite natural resources of the Chesapeake and its surrounds. We can only influence the degree of withdrawal from our natural bank accounts, not the direction of the cash flow.

And so, the people keep on coming. The many uses and seductions of the edge, where land meets water, draw people so powerfully that nearly half the planet's population has settled on five percent of its land mass — the 5 percent that is mostly adjacent to coastlines. In the United States, fully three-quarters of us soon will live within fifty miles of an ocean or a Great Lakes coast. And the heart of the heart of all this, the bay with perhaps the greatest amount of shoreline edge for its size of any place on earth, is none other than the Chesapeake. Compare the ratio of our bay's shoreline to its length with almost any similar coastal water body in the world. Usually these others show an edge that is two, three, or four times their greatest width; but on the Chesapeake, the ratio is nearly 35:1.

If humankind, concerned about a global population well on its way to doubling, were to order up a test case of how intensely we can exploit natural systems without irretrievably ruining them, we could have done worse than construct a scenario such as the one will be living out for the next several decades around the Chesapeake Bay. The population in the bay's sprawling watershed now is about twelve million people, with the bulk of them predictably clustered as close to the water's edge as they can afford. The modern history of our failure to stem the bay's environmental decline has been not so much a case of ignoring the adverse impacts of this population as it has been underestimating the rate at which changes were occurring. The population in the five-state watershed, which took 350 years of European settlement to reach 8 million people, required only thirty years more, the last 8 percent of our time here, to grow by 50 percent to 12 million; and we could double that within the lifetimes of many readers.

A similarly striking trend has marked our use of the watershed for agriculture, now recognized as a source of the rain-washed silt and chemicals that pollute the bay, on the whole, more than our sewage. At first glance, farming's impact appears to have decreased in modern times. Acreage in farms dropped a whopping 40 percent in Maryland alone in the last fifty years. But the soil that remained in the tillage has been pushed harder to extract ever greater yields. Use of nitrogen and phosphorus fertilizers, both major pollutants in the decline of the Chesapeake's aquatic life, soared by 250 percent per acre. The same thing happened in Pennsylvania, and, in an average year now, more than 80 million pounds of nitrogen and phosphorus are washed down the Susquehanna River alone. During the same period, equally rapid shifts were occurring from a farm economy based on livestock and pastures to one based on sowing grain crops. That meant more exposed soil washing into the bay. In 1982 the federal government confirmed that after fifty years of voluntary soil conservation, erosion from farmland stood at its highest rate ever. In Maryland in the latter half of this same period, the destruction of forests, which filtered soil and fertilizer pollutants from the runoff headed for the bay, proceeded at the highest rate in northeastern America.

The problem is not just more of us, but more of us each expecting more. Consider the impact on the Chesapeake Bay from an item at the center of the American dream, the home. In the decade 1970-1980, while Maryland's population grew by about 8 percent, the amount of undeveloped farm and forest required to house each person grew at triple that rate — clear reflection of the increasing demand for a rural or suburban home setting with a large lot. The more affluent new bay-dwellers were, the more they consumed the countryside of the watershed. Nearly two-thirds of all the land that changed from open to developed space went to house a mere fifth of the population growth. Most of this development took place on land outside areas where water and sewers were planned, mocking the "comprehensive land-use" plans county governments like to trot out as evidence they have achieved "controlled growth."

Other areas in which the desire for a higher standard of living exacerbates the impacts of growth are not covered by any plans at all. We do not usually even connect them as cause and effect. Yet just as surely as we all want more air-conditioning, more power plants on the water's edge are needed; and as each of us aspires to a boat (I have one, and *need* two more), we must have more and bigger shorefront marinas. And we all, quite naturally, hope someday to have a vacation home at the shore, or at least a vacation, which means more bridges and roads and cars to get there. Eventually, it all means fewer untrammeled natural coves in the shoreline and bends in the river.

It all comes back to wanting Frazee Ridge and Parramore Island, but, if you please, with a shopping center, good schools, and lots of modern job opportunities in close commuting distance — and while they're at it, can't they do something about traffic, which seems to get worse every year! More people, seeking the best of both worlds — and scarcely one among them does not earnestly subscribe to balancing the developed with the natural. It is a curious kind of balance, though, that must be refigured, however minutely, every time another soul is added to the watershed. Each time it is struck anew, we seem to be left with a little more concrete and a little less nature.

Now, I am optimistic that, with even a little luck, we will soon see some payoff in more fish and cleaner waters from the massive and technologically sophisticated Save the Bay campaign, on which the states of the watershed have launched themselves. But it is short-term optimism. Talk to the scientists whose research has laid the foundations for the next wave of pollution controls, and they will tell you that it will not be many years before the population trends and life-style demands again outstrip any gains. Many may say to that, "So what if they do?" We will be ready at that time to respond with whatever degree of bay-saving is required.

That is not such a bad approach to a number of ongoing problems, such as regulating the nation's money supply, or maintaining its road system. We operate that way often enough that a Yale economist, Charles Lindblom, even gave it a formal name, "muddling through," in a famous article published in the 1950s. At its best, Muddling Through recognizes that we are not really all that good at divining long-term, comprehensive solutions to problems — there are too many variables and imponderables involved. Instead, we make admittedly incomplete, imperfect decisions, followed up by almost constant, incremental midcourse corrections. It is essentially how we run this country, for all our talk about long-range planning.

But consider the flaws in Muddling Through if we really desire no further degradation (indeed, we want restoration) of the environment in the bay region. First, it is the character of an estuary, where rivers war constantly with the ocean for dominance, that the plants and animals living there routinely and quite naturally undergo dramatic declines and rebounds from year to year, as the dynamic environment there favors now this one, now that. Thus a true environmental problem usually is confirmed only after a downtrend is firmly established. The virtual disappearance, between 1969 and 1972, of the bay's submerged aquatic grass, one of the estuary's major life-support systems, did not begin to be sorted out from natural ups and downs until the late 1970s. It was around the end of that time that I shared a beer with Walt Boynton, a bay scientist with a remarkable gift for explaining complicated environmental problems to laypeople.

What did he think had happened to the bay grasses? I asked, knowing that research into the mysterious disappearance had just begun, but also knowing that no scientist heads into a project without some pretty good hunches, which they call hypotheses when they are seeking grant money. Walt sucked on his beer and said, after a long pause, "Too much shit and too much dirt is what I think it will turn out to be, but it'll be four or five more years before we can prove that to where anyone will be able to do something about it."

Walt was right on both counts. The killer turned out to be a combination of chemicals in treated sewage, combined with the same chemicals and the dirt washing off millions of acres of farms in the watershed. By the time Maryland, Virginia, and Pennsylvania had been convinced to make major commitments to control the problem, it was 1983; and, depending on which state one is talking about, it will be anywhere from 1988 to the end of this century before major reductions begin to occur in the pollutants that have been killing the bay's grasses. Thus, changing course in the way we use land and water across an immense watershed can take a generation or more. And during that time, causes of the problem continue. It is one reason we end up "progressing" at William Hargis's three knots against that unrelenting five-knot current.

Similarly, as we turn the watershed increasingly to human use, we permanently foreclose valuable options for reversing pollution. On the Patuxent River, at 110 miles the longest waterway wholly contained in Maryland, it was determined a few years ago that in dry summers treated sewage from booming upstream growth centers would soon make up around 75 percent of all the fresh water flowing down the river, with implications for the rich seafood-harvesting areas of the lower Patuxent that made even the sanitary engineers wince. A bold commitment was made by upstream sewage authorities to quit using the river as a waste sink. They would begin to spray the sewage, after treatment, on the land, allowing the soil to filter out the final traces of harmful pollution. Environmentalists cheered. But it never came to pass. The region in question already had developed to the point that the considerable acreage required for spraying the sewage simply could not be assembled.

Finally, we have always put a good deal of faith in the bay's resilience, its ability, given half a chance, to recover from environmental insult. Our faith is not without a basis. When the Chesapeake Bay Foundation was making a movie about the bay recently, there was an office joke that it could not decide whether to call it *Fragile Paradise* or *Sturdy Sewer*. So many times in recorded history, this or that species has been knocked back by natural events or pollution, only to resurge to record levels. You wonder at all that we have wrecked in the bay's environment; but even more, you wonder at how much survives.

Yet, if we look at the bay's natural defenses of a century or two ago, we must recognize that, like any veteran of many tough rounds in the ring, our Modern Chesapeake has lost forever the ability to take a punch like it once could. Consider the haymaker delivered by Tropical Storm Agnes in late June of 1972. The worst flooding in perhaps two centuries across most of its huge watershed blasted the estuary for days on end with unheard-of volumes of choking silt, farm chemicals, sewage from ruptured lines, and fresh water — the latter as deadly a pollutant as any of the others to salt-loving aquatic species. Agnes would have been a rude shock to the Chesapeake's system in any age, but, coming in modern times, it almost surely was far more devastating.

The forest — which once covered virtually 100 percent of the watershed, unsurpassed among all types of land use in filtering pollutants and absorbing the runoff from storms before it reached the bay — had been reduced to nearly a third when Agnes hit. Similarly the bay's stocks of oysters, once so vast it is estimated they could filter and cleanse the bay's entire volume through their gills every week or so, were now reduced to perhaps five percent of their former glory. The great reaches of underwater grasses, which had existed continuously in the bay for at least one thousand years, were already highly stressed by pollution when Agnes hit. They never bounced back, and with them went their ability to absorb several sewage plants' worth of nitrogen and phosphorus, two chemicals that have increasingly plagued the bay ever since. Fifteen years later, people will still say of this bay problem that, "Things haven't been the same since Agnes." The truth may be that Agnes wasn't the problem so much as the incapacity of the modern bay — shorn of its biological filters and buffers, destabilized and stressed already to the limit — to handle the insult.

Sometimes the loss of resilience has been more concrete. In the last century or so the bay has lost hundreds of miles of prime spawning rivers to big dams, notably on the Susquehanna, where rockfish once mounted as far as the Juniata, and shad and herring ran all the way past Binghamton, New York. As a result, the fish simply have a lot fewer windows at which to place their bets for a successful hatch. And in addition to the major dams we know about, it is estimated there are more than 900 blockages, small dams, culverts, and so forth, closing the innumerable miles of small spawning streams all over the bay region.

Breathing space for the bay to rebound has even been lost in court, as recently as the Bruce Decision in 1971, which released the watermen of every Maryland county to oyster and crab outside their county waters. It quickly created a more mobile work force, with bigger, bay-ranging boats that can now exert tremendous pressure within a matter of hours on any new "hotspot" where the beleaguered oysters and other species try to stage a comeback.

Beyond the loss of resilience that our demands on the bay have created is another type of pollution that should give special pause to the very people who rail the loudest against controls on growth and private land use. It is the loss of freedom, and it is the inevitable price that a civilized society exacts as it tries to infinitely expand the use of finite resources. Simply put, the more family that moves into your house, the more rules you all have to live by to keep from each other's throats. As Nick Carter, a minor philosopher and environmental permit writer for the state of Maryland, has pointed out, there are so many uses impacting the bay, the rivers, and the land that, to compensate, we regulate. Thus we now need a license to fish in the bay, a half-dozen stamps and permits to hunt; and we have rules that tell us what kind of detergent (nonphosphate) we can wash our clothes in, a soaring fee for boat registration, and serious talk of requiring licensing for boaters and creel limits on certain species of bay fish. If we double and someday triple the population in the watershed, I would expect lotteries to determine who got to camp on Assateague Island, shoot many species of duck, or take home a rockfish; and only cars with license plates ending in odd numbers will use U.S. Route 50 to the beaches on the first and third weekends of each summer month.

Will we save the bay? It seems unimaginable that we can restore it to any level of quality that existed much before the late 1950s. Even if the restoration could be done, the sacrifices would be too great, and I imagine the expectations of today's public would be mostly satisfied before that point. Most scientists I talk to think it unlikely we can do more than hang on to most of what we've still got left, and many feel all we can do is slow the present rate of decline. I sometimes remind people that if we even save half of what the Chesapeake is about during the next several generations, we'll still have more than most regions of the world.

I know from experience that this kind of speculation strikes the politicians and the bureaucrats as pessimistic, and smacks of criticism of their ability to carry out the public mandate, which clearly is to save the bay, but they miss the point, which is that so much of what is changing the Chesapeake simply remains beyond the current or envisioned scope of our political-legal system to deal with it. Doubters might wish to read the final report of the first modern bay conference held in 1968. It posed five basic policy questions which, had they been clearly answered, might have made it unnecessary to gather fifteen years later to plan one of history's largest environmental salvage operations. They asked, regarding the bay:

How many people do we wish to house on the shores?

How many tons of food do we wish to harvest, and what kinds?

How big a ship do we wish to accommodate (implications for dredging and dredge spoil disposal)?

How many pleasure boats will be operating?

How many acres of wetlands should we preserve?

We have not yet faced up to any of those questions, with the exception of wetlands, soon after protected by law, and are only beginning to recognize them as legitimate issues. How big? How many?

How much? Those questions seem almost to paralyze us, so directly do they suggest limits to our pursuit of the best of both worlds. They confront a faith in perpetual progress, reinforced by nearly two millennia of a Judeo-Christian tradition that sees the earth as planned for the benefit of humanity.

As a boy I listened as old market gunners on my native Eastern Shore cited Genesis, about the Lord assigning man dominion over the fish and fowl of the earth, to justify their inalienable right to continue slaughtering wild ducks without limit. Today, most of us chuckle at such attitudes, even as we shake our heads ruefully over the latest bulldozing for another road, or shopping mall, or sprawling housing development, and remind ourselves that growth, after all, is going to come whether we like it or not; and people do have the right to realize as much profit as they can get from their land. Sometimes people question whether it has to be this way; but they are easily dismissed by proponents of growth as having gotten their piece of the countryside, and now wanting to keep others out. I wonder sometimes whether the boomers of such continued progress wouldn't have sunk Noah's Ark, trying to add more cabins on the deck.

Will we save the bay? I know that we will always be trying; but "saving the bay" can become almost a state of grace, like tithing, allowing us to proceed comfortable with business as usual in the rest of our lives. My feeling is that we must broaden our definitions of environmental quality to include far more than the standards set forth in clean-water and clean-air laws. We must fundamentally reexamine our striving for the best of both worlds, for numbers without limit. There are signs that we are beginning to do so, but make no mistake; in our incipient efforts to grapple with limits in the watershed of the Chesapeake Bay, we are embarked on waters fully as uncharted as anything Captain John Smith encountered nearly four centuries ago.

* * *

A few years ago, I made my first trip to Martha's Vineyard to help deliver a boat back to the Chesapeake Bay. It was late autumn, nasty weather, and I ducked into a local bookstore to escape a rain squall. Signs in the window were touting "the Christmas season" on the Vineyard. The place, evidently, was on the verge of attaining enough popularity to shed the typical Memorial Day to Labor Day cycle of resort towns. The heady prospect of a year-round economy beckoned.

Inside, I was astounded by the quantity and quality of publications on Martha's Vineyard and its environs — coffee table books, poetry, history, diaries, essays, fiction, whaling, architecture, calendars. A number of the talented authors were people who "summered" on the Vineyard, I was told. Seldom has a small island been more thoroughly or lavishly celebrated, I thought.

Later, I began to realize what that really implied. To produce and support such a body of local literature and photography absolutely required a community grown large and affluent enough to have supplanted much of the original Martha's Vineyard. If a lot of what used to be there hadn't vanished, would there be the nostalgia necessary to sell half the attractive volumes on display — or the stimulus to undertake them?

Anyone who is more than a casual browser in Maryland book stores will note that literature and photography of the Chesapeake have begun to flourish in recent years, even as the bay and its old life styles have continued to erode. I told all this to my good friend Tom Wisner, the bay folksinger, poet, and storyteller. He sent me a graph, which he said charts a prosperous, if remorseful, future for writers like me.

So, I hope you have enjoyed reading these words, friend, as I have enjoyed writing them. But let's have no illusions about the process we're both part of.

THE CONTRIBUTORS

JOHN BARTH, one of the pre-eminent writers of our time, was honored with a National Book Award in 1973. He is the author of eight novels, three volumes of short stories and works of literary criticism. He is the emeritus professor of English and creative writing at Johns Hopkins University.

ROBERT DAY, author of the novel *The Last Cattle Drive,* is a frequent contributor to *The Washington Post Magazine.* He is a professor of English literature at Washington College, where he is also the Director of the college's Literary House and of the Literary House Press.

DAVID FINKEL is a staff writer for *The Washington Post Magazine.*

BILL GIFFORD is a free-lance contributor to *New Republic, Rolling Stone, The Washington Post Magazine* and other publications.

RICHARD HARWOOD is an editorial columnist for *The Washington Post,* a former Deputy Managing Editor of that newspaper, and is now Executive Editor of the Literary House Press.

TOM HORTON, a columnist for the Baltimore *Sun,* is the author of *Bay Country* and other works on the culture and ecology of the Chesapeake Bay.

Anne Hughes Jander wrote her memoir of family life on Tangier Island during World War II and the post-war period more than forty years ago. It was published by the Literary House Press in 1994, long after her death, as *Crab's Hole.*

Eugene J. McCarthy, the author of more than a dozen books of history, poetry and essays, was a United States senator from 1959 to 1970, and was a Democratic candidate for president in 1968.

William W. Warner, for many years an Assistant Secretary and a consultant at the Smithsonian Institution, is the author of the Pulitzer Prize-winning *Beautiful Swimmers.* He has been a contributor to *Atlantic Monthly, The New York Times* and other publications.

Jonathan Yardley, principal book critic and a columnist for *The Washington Post,* was awarded the Pulitzer Prize for criticism in 1981. He has published five books, most recently *States of Mind: A Personal Journey Through The Mid-Atlantic.*